T0114992

The
MIND GATE
Process of
Empowerment

Experience the Awesome Power
of Your Subconscious Mind

Dr. Mitchell Mays

BALBOA.
PRESS
A DIVISION OF HAY HOUSE

Balboa Press books may be ordered through booksellers or by contacting:

Balboa Press
A Division of Hay House
1663 Liberty Drive
Bloomington, IN 47403
www.balboapress.com
1 (877) 407-4847

Because of the dynamic nature of the Internet, any web addresses or links contained in this book may have changed since publication and may no longer be valid. The views expressed in this work are solely those of the author and do not necessarily reflect the views of the publisher, and the publisher hereby disclaims any responsibility for them.

The author of this book does not dispense medical advice or prescribe the use of any technique as a form of treatment for physical, emotional, or medical problems without the advice of a physician, either directly or indirectly. The intent of the author is only to offer information of a general nature to help you in your quest for emotional and spiritual well-being. In the event you use any of the information in this book for yourself, which is your constitutional right, the author and the publisher assume no responsibility for your actions.

Any people depicted in stock imagery provided by Thinkstock are models, and such images are being used for illustrative purposes only. Certain stock imagery © Thinkstock.

Printed in the United States of America.

ISBN: 978-1-4525-8850-6 (sc)
ISBN: 978-1-4525-8851-3 (hc)
ISBN: 978-1-4525-8852-0 (e)

Library of Congress Control Number: 2013922543

Balboa Press rev. date: 04/17/2014

CONTENTS

Dedication ix
Acknowledgements.. xi
About the Front Cover xv

Chapter 1: A Common Condition................... 1
Chapter 2: A State of Mind 20
    The Cloak Room (State of Joy)............... 20
    The Law of Attraction 23
    Emotional Tone Scale 24
    Two Feelings.. 24
    The Diagnosis (State of Fear)................. 26
Chapter 3: The Mind Gate 36
    Our Identifications 38
    Theory of Mind 39
    Human Radio Transmitter 67
Chapter 4: Mastering the Emotional Tone Scale........... 70
    The Emergency Brake 77
    Mat Work.. 80
    The God List 81
    Unwinding Negative Energy.................... 83
    Pleasure and Pain—Upgrades................. 84
    Vision Boards & Mind Movies 88
    Affirmations and Reframing 92

Literal and Inferred Affirmations 93
Testing the Power of an Affirmation 94
Self-Talk 95
How to RESTORE an Emotional Tone 95
The Escape Button 96
Reducing Fear and Guilt 97

Chapter 5: Imagination 103
The Power of Suggestion 103
The Best Times to Do the Process 105
Alarming Awakenings 108
Hitch Hiking Ghosts 110
Emergency Backup Picture 111
Fantasizing 111
Images and Patterns 113
A Sure Sign It's Working 114
Feel It in Your Body 116
The Nature of Reality 116
What Does Visualization Do? 120
Quantum Computer Model 123
A Central Idea 125
Sixty-Eight Seconds 126
Monkey Mind 127
Hypnotherapy 128
Why Raise Our Emotional Tone? 130
The Secret to Getting What You Really
Want 130
The Deeper Secret 135
The Balloon "Guided" Visualization 136
Guided Imagery 144

Chapter 6: The Process 148
Intention 149
The Process 152

Breathing 154
Visualize 155
Anchor 156
Monkey Mind 160
That's What I'm Talkin' About 160
Commitment 162
Mind Gate Music 163

Chapter 7: How to De-Hypnotize Ourselves 165
Move Your Body 169
Count Yourself Out 170
A Breath of Fresh Air 170
Eat to Prevent Anxiety and Hypnosis 171
A Word About Water 178

Chapter 8: Who and What We Really Are 182
Energy and Creation 183
Overpopulation 187
Quantum Physics 188
What You Need To Know 189

Chapter 9: Channeled 194
I Am 195
The Dreamer 200

Chapter 10: The Process In a Nutshell 205

Some final thoughts. 209
Resources 213

DEDICATION

This book is dedicated to my wife Terri, who is my best friend and partner in this lifetime and probably in many others. She has always been my 'main muse'. You are, without a doubt, the most amazing person I've ever known and, to say 'I love you' becomes just words compared to what I feel.

ACKNOWLEDGEMENTS

First and foremost, I want to thank my life's partner Terri, without whose patience and persistence by dragging me, *kicking and screaming* into new experiences and adventures throughout our married life, I would probably never have written this book. She has truly been my muse for most of life and the devil's advocate at other times. She has always remained steadfast in her love and support of my creative endeavors.

To my parents, Loren and Myrtle Mays, who always believed in me and even though they had many of their own challenges in life, were always there when I needed them to help me through many of mine. Even though you have both transitioned to *the other side*, I know you are reading these words as I write them. I love you both and thank you for all the opportunities you gave me.

To the two angels on the road that night who kept me safe in one of my darkest hours.

My stepson Robert deserves special thanks for encouraging me to continue my writing and always having a beautiful positive attitude and words of encouragement to both his mother and me, and always, at the right time.

To my friend, Dallas Daniel; thank you for literally being there when I needed you most.

To my children, Venessa and Aaron; I am so proud of you both for overcoming so many obstacles in your lives and that you have risen above them to even thrive and accomplish so much. I am excited to see what else you will do. Special Thanks to: Kenn O'Neal and Connie Mei for their graphic designing wizardry. And also, to poppa Ken for being my friend.

Mario Duguay for the amazing art on the cover of this book (see ABOUT THE FRONT COVER).

"Thank you" could never express the love and gratitude I feel for the following chiropractors who gave of their time, their hands and their hearts unselfishly and without pay to tend to my practice and my patients when I was disabled and incapacitated. You have been—and still are my "brothers in arms" and did not let me down when I was wounded but lifted me up when I became weary of the fight; Dr. Robert Carloni, Dr. Joseph Schaffhausen, Dr. John Arishin, Dr. Gregory Smith, and Dr. Thomas Clarke.

So much gratitude and heartfelt love goes to my other angels who supported me physically, as well as spiritually, during the long months of rehabilitation; Sue Kessler, Kari Boss and Lola Garza.

A special thanks to June Milligan, Donna Hamilton, George Kappas and all my teachers at Hypnosis Motivation Institute without whose wisdom and skills I might never have understood— so well—the power of the Subconscious mind.

A very special thanks—to Kari Boss—because of her relentless streak of positive attitude and a love for helping others. A special thank you to my long-time (probably multiple lifetimes) friend-Lin Bixby—who tested my professional skills and *stirred* and helped awaken—many of my dormant spiritual attributes and capabilities.

And finally, I would be remiss if I failed to thank all the people in the small Eastern Sierra Valley town of Loyalton—who gave of their time, their food and their love to Terri and I. Thank you for sharing your lives with us.

ABOUT THE FRONT COVER

Mario Duguay is a *visionary* and a *messenger of light*. These words have been used to describe both he and his art. He captures the essence of the human spirit as one of *light* or pure energy. This is why I've chosen his art for the cover of this book.

The name of the painting on the front cover is called "Here and Now"— which captures the essence— of *my* work. When I found this image on the internet, I was looking for something that represented some of the central ideas I have written about in my book and I believe I found it in *Here and Now*. Mario's painting inspired me for months when I was writing *The Mind Gate Process of Empowerment*. When I would meditate about the book coming together I would envision the front cover with this art.

As I was getting ready to send the manuscript and materials to my publisher, I suddenly realized that I had not gotten Mario's permission to use his art. In fact, at that point I didn't even know who or where the artist who signed his painting simply as *Duguay* was. I then went on a search to find him. I eventually found Mario's website and his email.

I then wrote a lengthy email to him expressing how I admired his art and wanted his permission to use it for the cover of a book I'd written. As I sent the email off I would like to say I was hopeful for a positive response but two weeks later I had not heard back from him.

Checking in with my emotional tone guidance, I realized I had sent off my email to him *worried* that he may not respond or that it would be out of the question. Three weeks had passed and as I was doing some final edits and gathering my other images together, I began to feel less and less confident about having Mario's painting on my front cover. I began looking through images that my publisher had available as alternatives— but nothing grabbed me or resonated with me like Mario's— *Here and Now.*

In my meditative visualizations and plastered all over my home office walls was *Here and Now* with the words *The Mind Gate Process of Empowerment* typed above it. I had copied and pasted the painting and even made a mock book cover with it and— in my heart I knew—there had to be a reason for this image coming to me. Just a few days after my *self-imposed* deadline to send my publisher my manuscript and all the other images that had to go into the book, my wife suggested I email Mario again from my other emails (I have six total). Because, she reasoned, maybe my first email went into Mario's junk email box.

As I began to release all the *disappointment* and *worry-energy* around having—*Here and Now* for my books cover— I began to feel much better. So then I thought— *okay, why not, I might as well have fun with this.* So, I copied and pasted the original email letter I had sent Mario to my other five email addresses and sent them off again—to Mario. I began musing to myself and thinking that I could send them again after being translated into French— if I don't hear back from him. There was a lot of *love*-energy flowing to Mario because he would be getting my email where I was singing his praises in my letter— times six!

Two nights later when I checked my other emails my heart began to sink just a little because there was no response from Mario but when I checked the last one (the email address I rarely use), there in my inbox was a response from Mario saying— "yes" he would be happy to sell me the rights to use his painting for my book.

I shouted with *joy!* "Yes" I said out loud, "Yes, yes, yes." I sprang from my computer shouting excitedly to my wife; "I got an email from Mario and he said he would give me permission to use his painting on the cover of my book!" "Yes, yes, yes" and we hugged, sharing the moment in gratitude. "Thank you, thank you, thank you" I said to my higher power, *Thank you—thank you—thank you.*

Look at **The Emotional Tone Scale** in Chapter 2. I want you to understand the dynamics of what happened here.

When I sent the first email to Mario I was already having *doubts* because— I was thinking about how *disappointing* it would be if I didn't have his painting on the cover of my book. From there, my emotional tone had already skated down to *Worry* by the time I clicked the *send* button. I continued in the emotional state of *Worry* until— I finally decided to leave it up to the *universe* and— just have fun. After all, I thought, *it's my message that's important, not the cover of the book.* Then I thought— at the very least— the artist named Mario Duguay might be amused by my persistence. The thought of him chuckling as he read my emails— pulled me right on up the scale to *Happiness.* That shift in emotional gears— shifted the energy— rapidly— around the whole project.

You see? It's so simple!

CHAPTER 1

A Common Condition

"Your time is limited, so don't waste
it living someone else's life"
–Steve Jobs

I have been working in health care for over thirty five years as a licensed chiropractor and a certified medical hypnotist. I have observed and treated, both as a chiropractor and a hypnotherapist, *a common condition*. This *common condition* is a result of anxiety that is mostly chronic but often can be acute and very intense. It is known in hypnotherapy circles as a *trance* state or *waking* hypnosis.

This *tranced* state causes us to feel overwhelmed and often powerless to make the changes that we know deep inside— need to be made if we are to ever realize our full potential. *Information overload* and feelings of *overwhelm* lead to this *tranced* state and often manifest as various ailments including neck and back pain but—they are also responsible for most injuries and accidents that send people to emergency rooms— or even worse.

As a hypnotherapist, my first and foremost responsibility is to get my clients <u>out</u> of hypnosis and then teach them how to _stay out_ of hypnosis during the so-called— waking hours. Because clients are almost always in a state of waking-hypnosis or _trance_ the first time they see me, I have to take them out of hypnosis before I can put them back into hypnosis— so that I can _install_ positive ideas and suggestions for the changes they want—into their Subconscious mind. As crazy as that may sound, my colleagues have the very same experiences with their clients.

I had observed this tranced _phenomena_ for many years in my patients— and just about everywhere else but— until the night of February 23, 2010—when my life would be changed forever— I did not fully understand how dangerous and devastating it could be. My wife Terri and I were getting ready to leave our office near Lake Tahoe in the mountain town of Truckee. It was getting late and I was feeling significant anxiety because we had a one hour drive ahead of us to our home, north of Truckee, and, it was beginning to snow. I was finishing up with my last patient and looking out at the snow from my treatment room window. It was showing no signs of letting up.

My heart was beating faster and my face flushed as a feeling of dread began to move up from my stomach to my solar plexus. I fought to push it down but —it was too late. My sympathetic nerve system's fight or flight response had been triggered. As my receptionist and my wife Terri were finishing up with shutting down the office, I stared out the window at the steady snowfall. My anxiety had now elevated to mild panic as I hurried to get the last patient out the door so we could close up the office and get on the road.

We were putting on our ski jackets and loading the office laundry and our assorted bags of paperwork into the four-wheel drive Toyota Tundra when the snow began coming down in big soft fluffy flakes—at an ever increasing rate. We quickly finished loading the Tundra, locked the front doors to the office and then, settling in for the long drive home, we drove out of the parking lot and onto the road that lead to Hwy 89 going north— to the little mountain community of Sierraville.

That night, and on one of the most dangerous twenty-five mile stretches of mountain highway in the state of California, all the cars were moving cautiously at twenty five to thirty miles per hour. The white and yellow lines on the road were being quickly obscured by the big, sticky snow. The temperature of the road was low enough not to melt the falling flakes and it was accumulating fast as the storm brewed. The pine trees on each side of the road were now frosted by an ever-thickening layer of new snow with each mile we drove.

My feelings of fear had now risen to a level probably not unlike those of a soldier who would be going into battle— at any moment. I was hyper-vigilant and prepared for all possible scenarios—and the heavy, wet Sierra snow slowly and steadily gathered depth. Terri and I were used to driving in *snow-country* because we had lived here nearly fifteen years but— this drive— on this night was somehow, different.

Many times and for many years we had driven over thick ice and heavily snow-covered highways— even in blizzards and *white-outs*. Many times, and for many years I had always felt some anxiety or what I would think of as— healthy vigilant awareness —but never had I felt such a *gripping terror* arising from deep within me like I did on this particular night. I had been dreading the day when the snow would come and I would have to make that drive for nearly two years and now— it had finally arrived.

Two years earlier, we had moved from our home in Truckee to the northeast Sierra Valley. We had decided to move to the Sierra Valley for several reasons, not the least of them being the cost of living which is much lower than Truckee and Reno, but, the incredible beauty of the Sierra Valley is breathtaking. Later we would come to know that the people that live there—are much like the land. We had both felt that the fifty plus minute commute would be worth it because we had already established a small practice in the town of Loyalton. Loyalton is almost exactly half-way between Truckee and Reno, where we did most of our shopping. So, after moving our home we had expanded our lives and made new friends, once again.

But this night would be the first time in nearly two years of commuting to and from Truckee that we would be driving home—on this particular road—during a snow storm. We frequently saw patients up until seven pm so our custom was to stop and get a protein snack before making the commute home, even if it was just a *taquito* from the local Taco Bell— but not this night. I was feeling such an urgency to get on the road before the storm got worse, we did not stop to get our snack. We had gone too long without eating and were cranky with the weather and each other.

As we drove on, our moods were not improving. We both were watching the snow falling as it was steadily increasing. There were several other commuters driving behind us that night and we were all driving slowly, up and down and around blind curves of treacherous Hwy 89. The snow continued to fall more heavily. I drove as attentively as I'd ever driven during a snow storm on mountain roads, without talking, until about half-way into the twenty-five mile stretch between Truckee and Sierraville.

Approaching one of the worst parts of the road near Sage Hen Creek we both saw the headlights of a vehicle driving around the curve in the road, up the hill, ahead of us. Through a *veil* of falling snow the lights moved eerily—across the road like a ghost or spirit crossing a room and then—as if suddenly aware of our presence—turned and headed right toward us. The headlights of this *phantom-vehicle* were now pointing down the hill in our direction. My foot stepped on the brake pedal as I began pulling over to the right side of the road—as far as I dare.

"I think he's in our lane!" I said incredulously. I watched in utter disbelief as the headlights were now aimed directly at us— and coming fast.

"He *is* in our lane" Terri cried out— pushing her feet hard against the floorboard of the Tundra—bracing for the impending crash.

Our truck came to a near-stop I was still hoping this *ghost-vehicle* would correct in time and miss us. The Tundra stopped with my right foot jammed down hard on the brake and my hands gripping hard on the steering wheel— I braced myself for the inevitable impact and then— the headlights found us. My fears about making that drive in a snowstorm had become a terrible reality in the form of a *head-on* collision!

Our truck's interior cab light was lit when I noticed the deflated airbag draped *limp* over the steering wheel. It was strangely quiet as if I had cotton stuffed into my ears. My head pounding as I surveyed the cab—as if in slow motion— to my right and toward my wife.

"Are you okay?" I asked.

"I think my leg is broken", Terri replied. "It feels like there's cold water running from my knee and down my leg."

I remember feeling relieved that she was conscious.

"Are you bleeding?" I asked.

"I don't think so", Terri gasped.

I reached over to check her left leg for bleeding as my right foot fell off the brake pedal. I felt a horrible grinding in my lower leg and no sensation of a foot being attached there.

"My leg is broken" I said as a matter of fact— not registering the implications or the severity.

"I think my right ankle's broken too", Terri groaned.

"Oh my God", I exclaimed.

I don't know how Terri had the presence of mind to do this but, she reached into her purse and retrieving her cell phone— dialed 911. There had never been cell phone reception in this section of the highway but, for whatever reason on this night— she got through and spoke to a dispatcher.

"Where are we?" Terri asked me urgently.

"I don't know exactly" I said—looking at my left wrist for the watch that was no longer there. Terri was talking to the dispatcher on her phone and trying to guess where we were. I don't remember what was being said.

I still don't know to this day how much time had passed before I was aware that someone was pounding on my side window. There were rushing sounds like *heavy surf* in my ears as I struggled to stay conscious.

"Open your door!" a woman was shouting from outside, "Your truck is smoking badly and might catch fire…you've got to get out!"

"Get my wife out first", I shouted back at the woman through the glass.

"We tried— the door won't open", she replied.

"Okay", I said, but my door latch was not working. "It won't open!" I said as I began frantically to pull at the door latch.

"Push against the door and we'll pull" she urgently shouted back at me.

I pushed the left side of my body hard against the truck's door, feeling nothing as my upper body slammed against the door while lifting the latch and then, suddenly, it reluctantly popped open a few inches as it stiffly moved open a bit more, all the while making creaking and grinding sounds as if the hinges had been rusted shut. When the door finally opened I looked out and saw two women in winter coats as the snow continued to fall, heavier now.

"Get out—they shouted in unison—your truck is catching fire".

"My leg is broken— I can't walk on it", I replied.

"We have to move you away from the truck—we'll carry you—hang onto our shoulders".

I turned my body to the left, feeling my right foot drag across the floorboard—limp— as the nauseating grinding in my lower leg reminded me of the severity of the fractures that were just now becoming real to my conscious mind.

At this point I would have welcomed the bliss that severe shock would bring with its attendant unconsciousness—but I also knew that I could not let that happen. I had to be assured that Terri was safe and being tended to. The two women struggled to act as human crutches as I hopped slowly on my left leg across the snowy-covered road and away from our smoking vehicle. I heard the woman under my right arm suddenly scream out.

"He's not going to stop!"

I glanced to the right in the same direction she was looking and I saw the white pickup truck coming too fast down the grade and heading right toward us.

"He's going to hit us", the other women shouted.

I was now rolling down a steep snow-covered grade to the sounds of metal colliding into metal—then loud shouting and screaming.

"That sounded like two impacts" I thought to myself when I had finally stopped sliding down the steep ridge. I then realized what had happened. The two women had thrown me over the side of the road and saved me from certain death as the vehicle that had hit Terri and I head-on—was hit by the white pick-up truck. The white pick-up truck had then slammed the *ghost-vehicle* back into our truck where—Terri was still sitting, waiting for help.

I struggled to climb up the steep ridge and strained to listen to what was happening on the road above.

I was praying to God out-loud now—"please, oh please, oh please let her be okay, let her be okay", over and over again but the incline was too steep to climb where I had finally stopped sliding. My right leg was useless so I *crabbed* my body to the right using my arms and left leg to move to where the incline was less steep.

After several minutes of crawling sideways I could finally see the road and made my way up to the shoulder. I listened intently for the sound of Terri's voice—but all I could hear was a man screaming and shouting profanities over and over until I heard another male voice shouting back at him.

"Shut up!" "Shut up!" That voice was mine—I only had ears for Terri's voice.

"Let her be okay, let her be okay" I kept saying—over and over as I pulled myself toward the road.

When I neared the road, crawling on my belly toward a road-marker pole— I watched in amazement as a Jack Russell terrier trotted down the snowy highway, going south, away from the wreckage—right in front of me. I reached out and grabbed onto a road-marker pole. Using the pole as a crutch, I pulled myself up and onto my left knee and then up onto my left leg while my right leg hung above the road. I was looking to see if I could determine where Terri was.

I called out "Terri, Terri?" The two women who had thrown me over the road and into the crevice apparently had been looking for me and now were walking quickly toward me.

"Your wife is conscious— she's conscious—they assured me—they're getting her out now".

"Thank God—thank God" I said and as I hung limply on their shoulders my body began to shake uncontrollably.

My eyes searched the crash scene to find the Tundra. I then heard Terri's shouts and moans of pain as men were trying to move her out of the truck. Eventually the men got her out of the truck and were carrying her on a ski jacket that acted as a makeshift litter. I didn't know at the time that both her legs had been badly broken. They were carrying her back to a safe area, several yards behind our *downed* Toyota Tundra— on the mountain side of the highway. The Tundra sat still and helpless with its front end smashed up against its windshield. I would never drive it again—but it will always be a fallen hero to me because—it had saved our lives.

Once again the women acted as human crutches to take me back across the road to where the men were taking Terri. Once across the road they had me sit on the back of an *open-hatched* Subaru station-wagon while they removed the floor mat.

Another woman now helped move the floor mat and place it down on the shoulder of the road—maybe ten yards behind our truck. The men who were carrying Terri laid her as gently as they could onto the Subaru's floor mat. Then my two angels, disguised as women, helped me over to the mat to lie down with my wife until the ambulance arrived. Terri was lying on her right side, as she did when we slept with each other in our bed. I reached over with my left arm to hold her as I'd done thousands of times but— we were both shaking so uncontrollably that my arm wouldn't rest on her shoulder.

"Hang on—keep breathing" I said, over and over as we lay there shaking—together. Someone put a ski jacket over us. The snow kept coming down and fell onto our faces as we lay there together, shaking in the aftermath of the trauma and cold. When the paramedics arrived—they did their triage.

"Can you hear me—where are you hurt?" they called-out as calmly as they were trained to do.

"My right leg is broken and my wife's broken both her legs" I said with a shaky and raspy voice as though through a tunnel. They moved on to look at others who were hurt. I could hear them talking among themselves about our injuries and the others who'd been involved in the accident. I think I was the first to be lifted and then put into the ambulance. The paramedic in the back of the ambulance was trying to get an IV into me but was unable to get a vein.

"Where is my wife" I kept asking.

"They're taking care of her" he tried to assure me.

After what seemed like an hour he finally said, "They're bringing her up now". He was professional but was still very concerned and very kind.

"What's your name?" I asked, still fighting-off unconsciousness.

"Crash…they call me Crash".

"Well, that's apropos" I said and then his face lit up with a broad grin.

"They're bringing your wife in now sir".

"My name is Mitch" I said as I looked to my left to see Terri.

The paramedics carried Terri in on a *real* stretcher—placing her in the ambulance—beside me.

"Are you alright? I said to her through a fog and with a shaky voice—trying to hide my fear.

"I can't feel—anything" was her barely-audible reply. Within a few minutes we were making the slow trip to Tahoe Forest Hospital in Truckee. I remember the ambulance sliding quite a bit every now and then as the sirens blared—drowning out everything except Crash's voice occasionally shouting to the other paramedic riding in the ambulance and tending to Terri as we were driven to the hospital on the heavily snow-covered road.

I never knew until I had experienced it for myself—the human psyche can go through shock after shock after shock and never lose consciousness! We were both alive—but had suffered severe lower extremity fractures and multiple connective tissue injuries—to our necks and backs.

Over the next two years, and after multiple surgeries, physical therapies and self-rehabilitation— we had time to think a lot about how we might have attracted such a terrible negative experience into our lives. If it was *karma* as one of our spiritual teachers had suggested, then it must have been from some past-life.

It was not until I began to seriously study hypnosis and hypnotherapy that I finally found the answer I was looking for. So, how did I attract the experience of a terrible accident into my life? It was the emotional tone of Fear that I was not controlling, because I was in a state of hypnosis when we drove toward home that night. Too many hours without food combined with the anxiety I had about the drive left me *suggestible* to my own *thoughts* which eventually gained enough momentum to manifest a fearful event.

In Chapter 2: A State of Mind— I introduce you to the **Emotional Tone Scale.** Learning and then mastering this scale is the key to creating— anything you want. Not knowing about this scale can quite literally kill you— or worse. The emotional tone of *Fear* is at the bottom of this scale and leads to all sorts of bad stuff. You could think of it as *the dark side of the force* from "Star Wars." At the top of the scale is Joy— Love— Freedom and Appreciation. Learning to *hang-out* in these tones will create for you— anything you want because, this is where all the good stuff comes from.

I want you to know that all the *bad* or *negative* experiences that have *happened* to you— are because you are not controlling your state of mind and— staying out of hypnosis. You may not think you are in hypnosis— but I can assure you that, you are probably in hypnosis more often than not! I always ask my new clients if they have ever been hypnotized before. Most answer me "No". I then proceed to explain to them the following—"You have experienced being *in hypnosis*— lots of times."

For example— have you ever gone to a movie and even though you know it's not real, have found yourself *scared* or *laughing* or *crying* and not even noticing the person sitting next to you— munching popcorn? Movie producers and directors actually *count- on* us— going into hypnosis during the film. That's why the volume gets loud and the lights flash and the music is chosen very skillfully and carefully—to evoke a *mood!*

Or perhaps— you've experienced driving along a familiar route when suddenly you realize that you have missed the turn-off that you've taken many times in the past— but your mind was on something else.

How many times have you walked into another room of your house only to find yourself standing there—trying to remember why you walked into that room? Or maybe— you are looking frantically for your car keys and then realize they are in your hand! How many times have you said something inappropriate or not germane to a conversation and wondered to yourself— "Why did I say that?"

No— it's not just getting *old and forgetful.*

"We have been tranced from our social conditioning since we were small children", says Bruce Lipton, Ph.D. author of "The Biology of Belief" and "Spontaneous Evolution".

In his book "Ageless Body, Timeless Mind" -Deepak Chopra, M.D. remarks; "The number of impressions that get laid down inside us is staggering...behavioral psychologists have estimated that just the verbal cues fed to us by our parents early in childhood, which still run inside our heads like muffled tape loops, amount to over twenty-five thousand hours of pure conditioning".

Dan Siegal, M.D. who heads up the "MindSight Institute" at U.C.L.A.'s School of Medicine calls this *common condition* of tranced— "mind wandering." He considers this condition a destroyer of happiness. He says that neural-integration and "mindfulness" are the— *heart of health*! His work is called *interpersonal neurobiology.*

As a society, we are regularly bombarded by negative news on a worldwide scale. Disasters of all sorts, new technology that many cannot possibly keep up with, heavy commuter traffic, economic uncertainties, inflation, overpopulation, air, water and noise pollution to name a few. Societies, the world over are in a waking state of hypnosis due to an *overload* of information. This *overload* triggers our sympathetic nerve system to engage the body's fight or flight response —on a regular basis— which causes our mind to escape (flight) into hypnosis or trance and renders us hyper-suggestible. Our Subconscious mind then becomes vulnerable to all kinds of negative influences.

In his 1970 book, "Future Shock", Alvin Toffler popularized the term *information overload* to describe what happens to individuals and even whole societies when our *perception* is one of— too much change in too short a period of time. He named this overload a *psychological state of future shock*.

Toffler maintained that societies have undergone enormous structural change as we moved from an *industrial society* to a *super-industrial society*. The result being an overwhelmed society that struggles to keep up and adapt to all the changes as mental and emotional stress intensifies and becomes amplified due to our *faulty perceptions*. Toffler contended that this accelerated rate of technological and social changes generates people who feel *disconnected* and suffer from *shattering stress* and *disorientation*. Toffler's theory sounds a lot like being in a state of waking-hypnosis or *mind-wandering* to me.

Using hypnotherapy terminology— I could say that— our Subconscious mind is left unprotected when we go into an uncontrolled trance state because— the Critical area of our mind or the *mind gate* becomes *disorganized*. When our *mind gate* or *mind barrier* that normally protects us from too much negative information becomes disorganized— it opens up and it is no longer able to *critically analyze* the voluminous amount of information coming into our Conscious mind— on a daily basis.

Toffler's *psychological state of future shock* is so all-pervasive and inescapable in today's societies that it has become the norm by all standards. Aren't you totally amazed when you get a clerk or waiter that is not as least a little *zoned-out*? I would never belittle waiters or clerks of any kind because I worked as a clerk when I was doing my under-graduate work but— as we become more sophisticated as a society, we become even better at hiding our tranced states— and because nearly everyone else is tranced it seems normal to us.

What this means is that most people are not reacting or acting out of their logical adult conscious mind but rather are reacting to outside stimuli through a perception of reality that may be faulty or erroneous. We have all experienced this. When we are in a psychological tranced state— but unaware that we are— staying focused long enough to create or manifest our desires becomes nearly impossible because— we are easily confused! What's even worse is— we are easily influenced by all of the *negative* information we are subjected to on a daily basis. The *news* programs are the first things that come to mind for me. Do you still believe that news programming is unbiased?

When we are in hypnosis, these negative messages can then get downloaded easily into our Subconscious mind. This can begin a *negative feedback loop* of thoughts and feelings as some of our own negative *programs* get stimulated. Have you ever asked yourself why you like or dislike certain races of people? Have you ever wondered why your family-of-origin all seem to act out certain behaviors in similar circumstances or have *built-in biases*? Our families are not the only programming we have been subjected to over the years. Think of grammar school—or even Sunday school and what about the kids you hung-out with when growing up. As grim as this may sound there is hope. You can change your programming if— you can change your perceptions!

We must accept the possibility that a change of perception in regards to how we see both *ourselves* and *the world* is what it will take to make a significant impact on our physical reality. To get what we desire or want and to make *positive* changes in our lives— it is *vital* —and I do mean *vital* for us to learn how to stay out of and prevent trance states from occurring during our waking hours. The only exception to this would be when we want to *deliberately* send positive messages or positive images to our Subconscious mind— to produce *more* positive experiences in our time-space reality.

The Mind Gate Process is the *key* to you staying out of hypnosis and helping you attain the higher states of emotional feelings. These higher and more positive feelings or emotions are what *cause* the *attraction* of more positive people, things and circumstances in our lives. They are in fact, what determine our state of mind. The first time you reach these higher states of emotions like Joy—Empowerment—Freedom and Love using *the Mind Gate Process* you will experience what I call a *psychic* or *mind orgasm*!

This book will inspire you to:

- Get out of trance and prevent yourself from going back into trance involuntarily.

- Gain a working knowledge of the mind's magical and awesome creative powers to shift our *perceived* reality and halt the negative emotions that sabotage our lives.

- Practice using *the emotional tone scale* to get in touch with your *built-in guidance system* to subjectively test anything and everything— from the people you interact with to even your own inner dialogues so you can receive immediate feedback to confirm if you are— on the right path to manifesting your dreams and desires.

- Use your imagination—even if you think you don't have one—to create a powerful positive emotional transmitter that will attract literally—anything you want into your physical universe—including better health, vitality, friends, partners, wealth and peace of mind.

- Cleanup your negative energy and reclaim your personal power and vitality by controlling the *monkey mind* when you wake up your *gatekeeper*.

In **Chapter 2: A State of Mind**, you will become familiar with *the emotional tone scale* and two stories from my life that will illustrate just how our emotional states attract and even create the reality we experience—not the other way round.

In **Chapter 3: The Mind Gate,** you will gain an understanding of how you were programmed and then—how these *programs* create our emotions and our state of mind.

Chapter 4: Mastering the Emotional Tone Scale is full of valuable tools and techniques to help you *release* negative energies and influences to help you—attain and retain—the *higher* positive emotional states.

In **Chapter 5: Imagination**, you will come to know that your imagination is the most valuable and exciting faculty you possess. It is what makes being a *human being* insanely strange and wonderful! Even if you think you are unable to visualize—or think you may have lost the ability to imagine—you will find here the tools that will help you—restore and enhance—your mind's natural faculty or *power to imagine.*

If you can worry or experience the emotion of fear—then you can visualize and imagine. I also discuss in this chapter some ideas and techniques that have helped me and my clients to create a *frenzy* of positive emotions.

And, don't miss *The Balloon- a Guided Visualization.*

After reading through the first five chapters you will be ready to begin **Chapter 6: The Process.**

However, you will want to refer frequently to **Chapter 7: How to De-Hypnotize Ourselves.**

For an insightful and amazing *Course in Miracles- style* descriptive narrative of the tranced state of *information overload* that author Alvin Toffler described in "Future Shock", go to **Chapter 9: Channeled** and read *The Dreamer.*

For those of you who may want a more scientific explanation of why and how the process works, please read, **Chapter 8: Not Who We Are, But What We Are.**

I know there are some of you who will want to go directly to **Chapter 6: The Process,** and that is fine but— without a full understanding of how our state of mind and emotions create powerful electro-magnetic waves or energies that emanate from us and then— attract back to us people and things, health or disease, money or poverty, positive circumstances or negative experiences— you may be retarding— or even sabotaging your desire for positive change and *manifesting* what you really want. The *monkey mind* is clever so *arm* yourself with knowledge and understanding.

You Have Two Futures

In one future you will continue to experience pretty much the same of what you have experienced so far in your life— but it may get progressively worse. This future is guaranteed, if you choose to stay in *trance*.

The other future is only limited to your wildest imagination. This future is also guaranteed if you choose to *wake-up* and experience the power that is yours to claim as a child of the Universe. As you reclaim your birthright— this power eagerly awaits your *conscious command*.

"Choose wisely"-from "Indiana Jones and the Last Crusade"

Chapter 2

A State of Mind

*"When the student is ready,
the teacher appears"*
-old Zen saying

The Cloak Room (State of Joy)

When I was six years old, I entered first grade in the small town where I grew up. The town had a population of 750 and a grammar school from kindergarten through eighth grades. I was not very excited about learning in the atmosphere provided. In other words, the teacher was not the nurturing soul I had experienced in kindergarten. In fact, in my estimation, she was downright mean. When I think back, she seemed to me to be related to the Wicked Witch from The Wizard of Oz. Within a couple of weeks, I had copped a bad attitude toward the teacher. One day during spelling, she punished me for talking instead of printing my letters. I was talking instead of doing my work because I was unable to print my ABC-s the correct way.

I was printing them backward and *feeling* frustrated and tense, so I did what I usually did at home when I felt that way, I engaged and entertained. Of course, this tactic was not appreciated by the Wicked Witch of the West, who saw my coping mechanism as a disruption to her class and a flagrant demonstration of disrespect for her and perhaps the public school system as a whole. I don't know— how could I know honestly— what she was thinking. Maybe her marriage was stressful. Maybe her own children gave her grief. Maybe-- a thousand maybes—I forgave her many years ago.

All I remember is this-she was angry with me and spoke sternly about "paying attention" and then marched me to the back of the classroom, where the cloakroom was, and had me sit down by myself with the door to the classroom closed. There, supposedly, I was to contemplate my rebellious actions.

As I sat there *feeling* bad, I noticed the backdoor was open, and I also noticed it was a beautiful fall day with the sun shining and the birds chirping. At six years old, I knew that I would *feel* better going outside. It was easy for me to imagine being outside with the sunshine on my face, the smell of the valley oaks, the sounds of birds, and the feeling of happiness, in other words, the total experience of being alive. Even though I knew I would be in trouble if I left the building, I also had the knowing that what I was feeling, sitting there on the cloakroom floor was not good for me. After a few minutes, I decided that it would feel better, no matter the cost, if I went outside and away from the bad feelings I was having there in the cloak room. Something inside of me made me get to my feet and slip out the back door of the first grade building, which sat across from the back door of the kindergarten building, where I had so many fond memories just the year before.

Between the two buildings was a drinking fountain, which sat atop two circular pedestals made of concrete. It looked a little like a two-layer cement cake with a metal-and- porcelain candle in the middle.

Directly perpendicular from the drinking fountain and only twenty feet away from the fountain was freedom! The front gate on the tall chain-link fence was open. *Yes.* My heart leapt— as I sprang from the first grade building, around the drinking fountain, and through the gate. Soon- I was happy as the smells of the fall morning air filled my nostrils and I breathed the air of freedom into my lungs.

As I think back on that experience, I now believe that as I was sitting there on the cloakroom floor, I most likely imagined how it would *feel* to be outside. I know now that positive subconscious programs were stimulated by thoughts of happiness which my body reacted to emotionally (emotion = energy in motion) resulting in the behavior that made me get up and move my body right out the door. *Whew!* So how does all of this work again? My decision to have better -feeling- thoughts triggered a happy feeling and the law of attraction responded to create this beautiful experience of freedom for me. The law of attraction seems to be tied in to *how we feel!*

The Law of Attraction

The law of attraction has been stated in various ways but basically says that— *like t*houghts attract *like* events. More accurately— like *feelings*— attract like events!

"Find thoughts that feel good, because it is inevitable that you are going to be moving toward something".-Esther Hicks as Abraham

"The key to seeing the world's soul, and in the process wakening our own, is to get over the confusion by which we think that *fact* is real and *imagination* is illusion". – Spiritual Writer, Thomas Moore

"A mental image gives you a framework upon which to work. It is like the drawing of an architect, or the map of the explorer. Think over this for a few moments until you get the idea firmly fixed in your mind". -William Walker Atkinson

Look at the emotional tone scale below. You could call it the *feeling scale* or *state of mind scale* or *vibrational tone scale*. It has been called by all of these names and more. There are many such scales and some are extremely detailed but I feel the one I've outlined here is accurate and suitable for our purposes. The trick to manifesting anything lies below— on this scale. We must learn this secret before we can move forward.

Emotional Tone Scale

1. Joy— empowerment—freedom—love—appreciation
2. Passion for another—passion
3. Enthusiasm—eagerness—happiness
4. Positive expectation—positive beliefs
5. Optimism
6. Hopefulness
7. Contentment
8. Boredom
9. Pessimism
10. Frustration—irritation—impatience
11. Disappointment
12. Doubt
13. Worry
14. Blame
15. Discouragement
16. Anger
17. Revenge
18. Hatred—rage
19. Jealousy
20. Insecurity—guilt—unworthy
21. Fear—grief—despair—powerlessness

Two Feelings

"One could say that there are really only two feelings. One feels good and the other feels bad"- Esther Hicks as Abraham

I've provided the emotional tone scale simply to help you get back in touch with your *feeling -self,* which is what the law of attraction or—the universe or— God or— your higher self really responds to and then— mirrors back or sends you something *like* those feelings. You will learn how to control this scale and deliberately move up the scale to better feelings or better- feeling thoughts— which then produce better *feelings* which then attract people— things and circumstances that are *like* those feelings. Let me give you another example from my life of how our thoughts affect our state of mind or emotional tone.

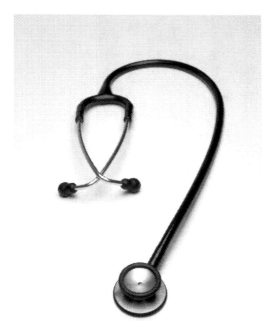

The Diagnosis (State of Fear)

In 1980, just three years after starting my chiropractic practice, I started experiencing pain in my lower abdomen that was not going away. I had struggled starting my practice, like most new professionals and my name was on the line for a lot of money. Between student loans and a business loan to start my practice, I had more debt than I ever thought possible.

The strain of realizing I was actually an entrepreneur in an industry in which I had absolutely zero experience and no idea how to ask or who to ask for help eventually took its toll on my state of mind. I felt the heaviness that comes with being in over your head. I literally felt gut-wrenching emotional pain because of the stress. I knew that I had bitten off more than I could chew. My business was just beginning to cover its expenses when my emotional pain became physical. I lived with it for about a month, and then it suddenly changed from a dull ache to a sharp stabbing pain.

My practice had just begun doing well, and I thought perhaps I'd overdone it when adjusting the spines of some of my larger patients. It was not a severe pain, but I thought I'd better attend to it. I went to a colleague, a fellow chiropractor, and asked him to x-ray my lower back and pelvis. When the x-ray came out of the developer and he put it up on the viewing box, I could hardly believe my eyes. I thought there had been some mistake and that this couldn't be my x-ray film. There in my pelvis, in the front where I had been feeling the pain, was a large bone tumor, about the size of a tennis ball.

My heart raced, and I felt my face flush. My pain suddenly stabbed me, as if to say, "See, I told you I was serious." I remember hearing myself asking him, as my heart pounded in my ears, what he thought it was. He said he didn't know but that he would have his associate take a look later and that I could call him later that evening. I felt my knees go weak and I felt as though I might pass out as my blood pressure climbed. I agreed to call him later and somehow stumbled out of his office. Driving back to my office the pain worsened—the stabbing pain coming more frequently now.

I had patients scheduled for the rest of the day, so decided to just go into denial, as I reasoned it would serve my patients better. My wife was working in my office and was at the front counter when I walked in.

"Did you get an x-ray?" she asked.

"Yeah" I replied trying not to let my face give away my fear. But it was too late; she'd read my face.

"Is something wrong?" she asked.

I was evasive and responded, "I don't know."

My head was spinning, and I was feeling a little queasy as I walked past the front desk and into my private office collapsing into my desk chair. She followed me in, and I related the story of the x-ray findings to her.

She tried to be positive saying, "Oh it's probably nothing."

If only that were true, I thought. I finished the day but struggled with each patient I treated, to push the image of the x-ray and the pain out of my mind. Before I left for home that day I called my colleague. His associate came on the phone. His associate was a chiropractic orthopedist with advanced studies in x-ray and orthopedic analysis.

"So what do you think?" I said in my bravest voice.

"Well, it doesn't look good", he said. "I think you should have a specialist look at it".

"What do you think it is?" I persisted.

"Honestly, I don't know" was his reply.

"Okay, thanks" hanging up the phone with a trembling hand. My wife had been listening to my side of the conversation and asked me what he thought "the thing" was. I related the conversation back to her. She was now beginning to lose her positive attitude.

The next day, I remembered that I had gotten spinal and pelvic x-rays eight years earlier by my old chiropractor. If he still had the films I thought, maybe he had missed it back then and there would be at least a shadow of "the thing" on the older films. This could mean that, whatever it was it may be old and there would be no need for alarm. I anxiously called his office to find out if he still had my films.

I was thinking, as his assistant went to ask the doctor about my old x-rays that maybe the tumor was there back then and he had missed it. Maybe it was a bone deformity from childhood. I was thinking about all the possibilities when his assistant came back on the phone.

"I'm sorry she said, the doctor says that all our x-ray films over seven years old were recycled. We don't have them anymore."

"Are you sure?" I asked. She put me on hold again but for just a minute when she came back on the phone.

"I'm sorry... the doctor says he is sure."

My heart sank along with my hope as the feeling of fear began creeping back in. I didn't want to see an orthopedic surgeon. I was scared to death and I was determined that I was going to "will" this thing away. The pain was not bending completely to my will after a few weeks but it had subsided greatly. I had reasoned that it could be something else besides a bone tumor. Maybe it was a prostate infection that only looked like a tumor. I went to my old family medical doctor and he checked my prostate.

"Yeah it feels pretty swollen" he said. "Let's get some fluid and look at it under the microscope and see what we have."

Now bear in mind, I was only 29 years old, but okay, if he thinks it may be a prostate infection, I'll take that any day over the alternative. When he came back into the exam room he said, "Well, there's no infection".

"What do you think it is" I stammered (I hadn't showed him my x-rays, nor did I let him in on the immediate past events).

"I don't know, shrugging his shoulders— but I think you should get a biopsy."

Finally, I had the courage to make an appointment with the orthopedic surgeon. The surgeon looked at the films, palpated my pelvis and said, "It looks a little like an "osteosarcoma"—but it's probably a good idea to get a biopsy." I really almost passed out with that remark. "Now don't let this interfere with your work", he tried to assure me.

Are you out of your mind, I thought. I had to cancel the rest of my patients that day. I could barely see to drive home and then could barely walk up the stairs to my apartment. When I had cleared my head and was finally able to read, I went thumbing through my pathology books under "bone tumors." No bueno news…if it were indeed an osteosarcoma type of tumor, I was a dead man walking. The anxiety rose again and so did my blood pressure to an even higher level. According to the latest information on that particular type of tumor and its location, I had less than a 2% chance of survival past one year.

As I read those words my fear went into overdrive and I escaped big time into my fight or flight response and then smack right back into denial. In short, I escaped into a tranced state or hypnosis. To preserve what sanity I had left, I had decided to just ignore it (since I was going to die anyway). Who knows, maybe I'll be one of the 2% who survive, giving myself encouragement while stuffing the fear.

After several months I was no longer able to push the pain aside and I couldn't stand living with the fear any longer. I was feeling a little hopeful because the pain was not worsening and I was still alive. I thought I'd consult a different orthopedic surgeon this time. While sitting in the exam room of the second orthopedic surgeon's office a few days later, I was getting more and more frightened as the pain was switching from stabbing sensations to a deep dull ache, then stabbing again as I watched his face looking at my x-rays. He had a very good "poker –face" from years of not telling people bad news unless he was "dead certain". I admired him greatly for that.

"Let's get some other x-ray views", he said. My hope elevated a tiny bit.

I had begun to calm down some when he came out to where I was sitting and signaled me come back into the exam room.

"I'm not sure exactly what this is", he said. "It does have some characteristics of an osteosarcoma". I almost fell off my chair as I became a little dizzy.

He noticed and quickly added, "There are lots of things that resemble osteosarcomas Mitch, so don't let your imagination run away with you".

"Too late", I almost blurted out loud. He was trying to reassure me and I felt myself beginning to move up the emotional tone scale a little from "dead meat" to "still alive." Maybe even a little more chance than 2% survival, I thought.

"I'll run these by some of my colleagues and get their input. In the meantime, I think it would be a good idea to get a biopsy." He got points from me by not saying "Don't let this affect your work". He knew I was scared but he also knew not to throw out answers until he had them and the tone of his voice helped calm me down. I was feeling a tiny bit better, not great, but better.

At his suggestion, and considering the location of the tumor, I made an appointment with a urologist for examination. After hearing the story, the urologist did a prostate exam.

"I think I know what it is but I'll call in my partner and get his opinion. If he concurs then we have our diagnosis". His partner (the other urologist) did yet another prostate exam on me and the two of them left me in the exam room while they went into the other room to talk.

Head spinning again I was beginning to feel even more ill than I was already. After conferring with his partner, he came back into the exam room.

"OK, let's schedule a biopsy." I didn't bother to ask what he thought "the thing" was and I probably wouldn't have heard him even if he had told me. Once again, I was in and out of hypnosis and fighting to keep my spirits up. I knew it would be a losing battle if I gave way to my fear again. I did everything I knew to do to feel better emotionally. I watched funny movies and played board games when I wasn't seeing patients. I hung onto hope with every ounce of courage I had.

A week later, I checked into the hospital for the biopsy procedure. It involved an overnight stay and numerous tests, intravenous x-rays with dye, chest x-rays, new pelvic x-rays, blood panels, etc. Under general anesthesia, my urologist performed a "needle punch" biopsy and within a few hours of regaining consciousness he came into my hospital room.

"Well, we still don't know what it is but I got a piece of it". I sat there speechless as he went on.

"The lab tests came back negative... it's not malignant." He had a smile on his face, the first one I'd seen since meeting him. It was a beautiful and radiant smile. Tears of joy filled my eyes.

When he left the room I sobbed with relief, releasing stuffed emotional tension that had been suppressed for so long. Wave after wave of emotion came up and then joy surfaced. I was thanking God over and over in my heart and mind. When I was able to reason again, I assessed and took stock of the situation.

What I knew at that point was, yes, there was definitely a tumor and it was large and it was hard, like bone, but here's the important part. My emotional state bounced up like a cork that had been held underwater and then released. As it bobbed to the emotional surface I felt waves of appreciation for life! I was still among the living and very, very happy to be so.

Everything suddenly looked different. From my hospital bed I noticed the bluest and most beautiful sky I could ever remember seeing. The grass was greener. The trees were awe-inspiring. There were dragonflies flitting around outside my window and I realized what amazing creatures they are. As I basked in this state of joy, I felt more alive than I had in years, so very much alive. The heavy cloak of the fear of death had been lifted from me. The nurses in the hospital appeared as angels ministering over me and welcoming me back to the living. I still didn't know what "the thing" was but I felt strongly that somehow, I would survive this.

About three weeks later, I received a letter from orthopedic surgeon number two. He wrote to me that he had sent my x-rays to a specialist in bone tumors in Oakland. There was a copy of a letter addressed to him from the specialist that read something like this, "**The tumor viewed on your patient, Mitchell Mays is not an osteosarcoma but is an osteochondroma. This one is quite large and is borderline malignant. I'll be happy to see him here in Oakland if you'd like.**"

To make a long story a little shorter, I checked into Kaiser Hospital in Oakland on Christmas day and the next day the tumor was surgically removed. The laboratory report confirmed it was not malignant.

Did the drastic change in my state-of-mind or my emotional tone, affect the outcome? I believe it did. I believe that, had I not faced my fear and moved up the emotional tone scale to Hopefulness (see emotional tone scale) when I went in for the biopsy and again moved up to Positive Expectation after the biopsy, I would not be writing these words today.

It took me nearly a year to learn how to walk normally again, but I progressed quickly considering the extent of the tumor's damage and the amount of bone from my pelvis that had to be removed. I know this, had I not been able to manage, at least to some degree, my emotional state of mind, I would have died.

It is critical that we learn how to manage our state of mind, in other words, really care about how we are feeling emotionally. It is also critical that we care about how we feel about ourselves! Typically we are mobile on the emotional tone scale. We are normally going up and down but it is where we chronically and habitually hang-out on the scale that is important here. If we are stuck in an emotional range, especially anywhere below Frustration, we will be attracting a lot of things into our lives that we don't necessarily want.

After you scan the scale, I will explain how our mind works from the point of view of a hypnotherapist. You should then have a much clearer understanding of why and how to manage your emotional states. Everything we want is dependent upon us doing just that!

So, the question then becomes— what seems to be your chronic (long standing patterns of emotions) emotional tone? And— do you have the power to control "it", or does "it" control you? Let's explore that, shall we? Now look at the emotional tone scale below again. Do you hang-out in a range of emotions or are you— all over the place?

Emotional Tone Scale

1. Joy— empowerment—freedom—love—appreciation
2. Passion for another—passion
3. Enthusiasm—eagerness—happiness
4. Positive expectation—positive beliefs
5. Optimism
6. Hopefulness
7. Contentment
8. Boredom
9. Pessimism
10. Frustration—irritation—impatience
11. Disappointment
12. Doubt
13. Worry
14. Blame
15. Discouragement

16. Anger
17. Revenge
18. Hatred rage
19. Jealousy
20. Insecurity—guilt—unworthy
21. Fear—grief—despair—powerlessness

CHAPTER 3

The Mind Gate

"Know thyself"
-Socrates

The following is a description of the *theory of mind* that many hypnotherapists, including myself, use with our clients to explain how our so-called thoughts—actually cause or create our state of mind or emotional tone. According to NLP (neuro linguistic programming) our state of mind or emotional tone is what *drives* our behavior. Our state of mind determines what things we pay attention to and how we either— react or act in various but consistent ways to what we have our attention on.

Our behavior is largely responsible for creating our reality by either *attracting* certain people, situations and things to us or by *repelling* certain people, situations and things away from us. Current research now validates how this mechanism works using *quantum theory* and *neuroscience*— but, I am not a quantum physicist nor am I a neuroscientist and chances are, neither are you. I will give you a *working model* of how hypnotherapists use this amazing mechanism we call the Subconscious mind because I believe that—one does not need to know how electricity works in order to use it, however fascinating it may be.

This is basically a cause and effect mechanism, only the cause is— for the most part— outside our *conscious* awareness. Some might describe it as the law of attraction and it most assuredly is that. It has been my experience and belief that the source of all our negative life situations and problems come from our Subconscious mind. As the Subconscious mind *bubbles- up* or sends thoughts to the Conscious mind— our body responds to these thoughts with emotion (energy in motion) and then we act on these emotions, or *behave* in certain ways. Response to stimuli is one of *the seven criteria of life.*

These actions or responses to the stimuli of thoughts in our Conscious mind and body are our behaviors. We may respond to thoughts in any number of ways— becoming irritable and angry or we may react with love and compassion. Why is this? Our emotions are responsible for creating our state of mind because we react to these thoughts as if they are *real* and—we never question where they come from. Worse still— we believe they are *who* we are.

We rarely question the legitimacy of these *thoughts* and *feelings*. We either feel good or not so good and often— do not even know or understand *why* we feel this way or that way. But, this is highly valuable information and is actually a kind of *built-in guidance system*. It informs us when we have jumped off the track and are heading where we don't really want to go. These emotions that come from our *thoughts* can cause us to *suffer* or cause us to want to *celebrate*.

While it is infinitely better to feel like we want to celebrate, if we're not sure or— don't know exactly how or why some feeling was created— we could have a problem.

For example— we may experience warm and fuzzy *feelings* when checking into a hotel and the valet reminds us of or looks a lot like mom or dad—we might *think* it was the valet who created these feelings in us. If we do not know about our Subconscious programs—we may behave in a manner that could cost us our marriage.

Our Identifications

All identifications (or attachments) to *forms* of any kind, cause suffering and this even includes *thought-forms*. This is what is meant by the second Noble Truth in Buddhism—

> "The origin of suffering is attachment to transient things (like the valet) and the ignorance thereof. Transient things do not only include the physical objects that surround us, but also ideas, and in a greater sense, all objects of our perception. Ignorance is the lack of understanding of how our mind is attached to impermanent things, including or especially thought-forms!"

The good news here is that while our Subconscious mind is the source of all our problems— it can be re-programmed to be the source of all our joy! You just need to know how.

THEORY OF MIND

Ages 9-12
Mind Gate Formed/Developed

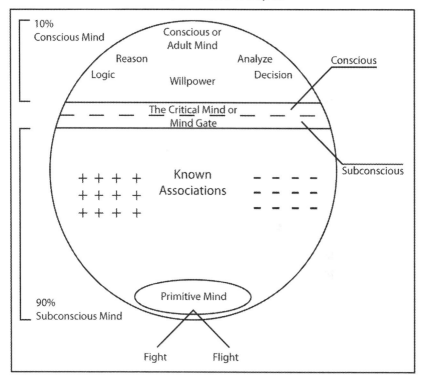

Fig. 1

Figure 1 represents a theory of mind that many hypnotherapists, including myself, use to explain how the *mind* works, to their clients. The circle represents our total mind and the area at the bottom is known as the Primitive mind. This is the part of the mind that triggers the fight or flight response when we are under extreme stress or facing a situation where we have to run or fight. Also inside the

Primitive mind are two primary fears, the fear of falling and the fear of loud noises.

The Critical mind resides in both the Conscious mind and the Subconscious mind. It has been assumed by hypnotherapists for many years that our Subconscious mind is about ninety percent of our entire mind and the Conscious mind is only approximately ten percent of our entire mind. Brain scientists (neuroscientists) and researchers are now estimating that our Conscious mind may be only five percent of our total mind! (When you realize that this is where our intellect resides it's a little humbling, to say the least).

It's extremely important to understand that our Subconscious mind does not think, nor does it reason or analyze. It uses no logical *decision-making* whatsoever. It is the Conscious mind or *Adult* mind that is all about reasoning and analysis, logic, decisions and willpower.

When we were very small, from age zero to eight years old, we took in information like a sponge. We absorbed this information through our five senses, the sense of taste, touch, auditory, visual, and olfactory or smell. All of this information and experiences became our "known" associations and identifications. In other words, the things we know about our world. By about age eight we have a library full of these *known* associations and identifications and our Critical mind then develops.

The Critical mind acts as a sort of barrier or filter to prevent any more new information or programming into our Subconscious mind without being critically analyzed by our Conscious mind first. We no longer accept any new programming at face value. This is when we begin to question information coming to us and also when we begin to control our state of mind and responses to stimuli or behaviors.

Age 0-8

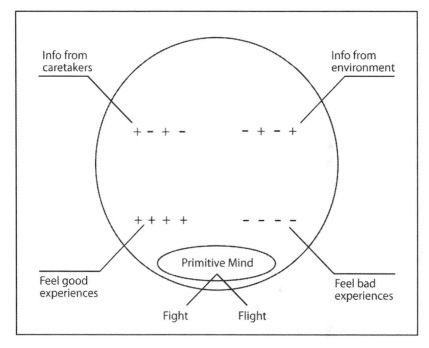

Info from caretakers

Info from environment

+ – + –   – + – +

+ + + +   – – – –

Primitive Mind

Feel good experiences

Feel bad experiences

Fight   Flight

Fig. 2

Figure 2 illustrates how this information comes to us mostly from our caretakers (usually mother and father) but between the age of zero and eight there could be several different people who are inputting information and experiences into your life. Siblings, aunts, uncles, grandparents, teachers, preachers, the environment and our own bodies all contribute to our "known" associations and identifications and, these associations and identifications can be positive or negative.

For example—if an older sibling is acting as a surrogate caretaker or is babysitting us quite a bit when we are small and is always telling us that we are—stupid—we will have a program (a known identification) that we are *stupid*. Later, when we are around that sibling or if someone we meet reminds us of that sibling, our *stupid* program may start running and we will feel *stupid* and not know why—or worse—we may grow up believing we are— *stupid.*

Another example could be when you were sitting in church as a child and the minister is telling stories about hellfire and damnation you may grow up believing that people who don't belong to your religion are all going to hell. But, many of these *known* associations and identifications or Subconscious *programs* can be fairly benign such as— hot weather *feels* bad or cold weather *feels* good or— a warm fuzzy blanket *feels* good and touching a hot stove *feels* bad but the smell of warm cookies in a hot oven *feels* good. A puppy dog may be a positive association— unless— as a child— a puppy dog's mother lashed out and bit you when you had reached out to pet the puppy— then a puppy may be a *negative* association. So, we have some *feel-bad* experiences and associations and we have some *feel-good* experiences and associations.

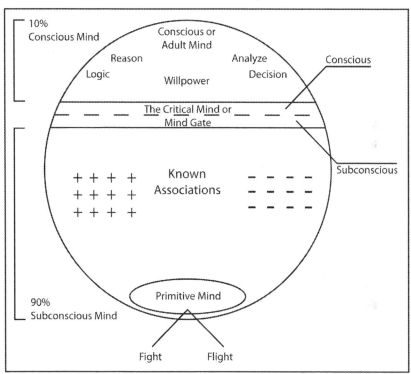

Ages 9-12
Mind Gate Formed/Developed

Fig. 1

Again, Figure 1 illustrates the Critical mind or what I call the *Mind Gate*. The Critical mind acts as a *barrier* to keep new information from filtering into the subconscious mind and creating new "known" associations or programs and, as stated before, the Critical mind is half in the Conscious mind and half in the Subconscious mind

43

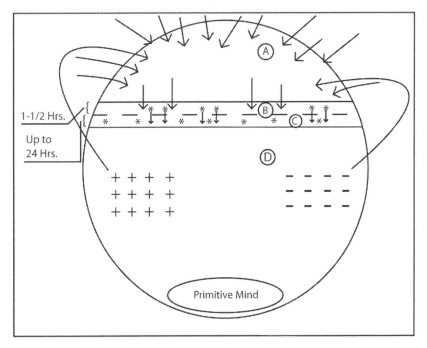

Message Units
from environment, our body and our subconscious

Fig. 3

A- Conscious Mind
B- Critical Area of conscious mind- Stores & analyzes data for up to 1-1/2 Hrs. then drops data (MU's) into C.
C- Critical area of subconscious mind- Stores & analyzes data during so-called awake state (16 Hrs).
D- Subconscious mind- Sends MU's in "thought form" to conscious mind.

Figure 3 shows us how information is coming into our Conscious mind. These bits of information are called "message units" and come from the environment, our own body and our Subconscious mind. The Subconscious mind sends or *bubbles* up information to the Conscious mind in the form of symbols or what we call our thoughts when its programmed *knowns* are stimulated. You could think of these *knowns* like computer programs with on-off buttons. When they get stimulated or switched on, the programs run —and when they are running they are sending symbols (message units) into our Conscious mind or awareness as thoughts.

If it is a *feel-good* program running, we will have good feelings associated with these thoughts. If it is a *feel-bad* program running then we will have bad feelings associated with these thoughts. For example—if you have been experiencing Fear, Grief or Despair frequently then your mind has been caught up in a *negative* program *feedback loop* where *negative* programs in the Subconscious mind have been stimulated. When these programs are stimulated they produce negative thoughts. When these thoughts reach your Conscious mind— your body reacts to them as emotions or feelings. We will go over these responses in great detail in the next chapter.

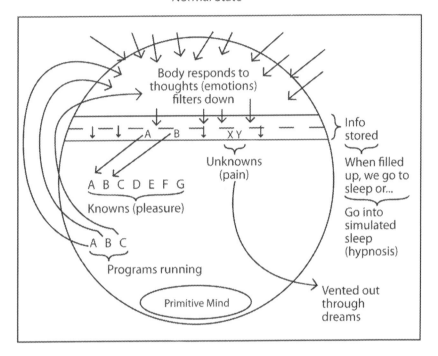

Fig. 4

When sleeping, mind gate opens & MU's drop through into subconscious (S.C.) if knowns. If unknown, they get vented out through dreams.

These Subconscious programs are constantly sending message units (MU's) back up to our Conscious mind when we are awake and are largely what we think of or call our thoughts. These thoughts gather in your Conscious mind in great numbers. Eventually they drop down into our Critical mind. Our Conscious mind only holds about one and a half hours of message units (MU's) before they settle down into the conscious part of the Critical mind for analysis. I like to think of this mechanism like a septic tank. As the waste water flows into a septic tank the solid waste eventually settle to the bottom.

Neuroscientists are now discovering that we are exposed to trillions of bits of information (message units) in the average day but that we are only consciously aware of a tiny fraction of that amount. All of that huge amount of information, whether we are aware of it or not, fills the Critical mind quickly. If we have a day that is filled with stressful information or experiences, we can get overloaded with message units (MU's)— within minutes and the Conscious part of the Critical mind then fills up and— will *dump* or drop its load of MU's down into the Subconscious part of the Critical mind.

There, in the Subconscious part of the Critical mind the information is analyzed for content and any of the information that is *like* any of our programs (our *known* associations and identifications) will be *earmarked* by the Critical mind as like our *known* programs and— those particular bits of information will stimulate and be added to those particular *known* programs.

All the rest of the MU's that are *not-like* or *unknown* to our Subconscious mind's programs will be tossed out in the form of *venting* dreams before we awake in the morning. Message units that are *known* represent *pleasure* to the Subconscious mind— even if they are bad for us (like smoking cigarettes). Message units that are *unknown* to our Subconscious mind represent *pain* to the Subconscious mind—even if they are good for us (like eating healthy food or exercising). Remember the Subconscious mind does not reason or analyze, it just plays back programs like a recording device.

Venting dreams are the dreams we experience and remember just before waking. All of the information that comes into our Conscious awareness has a way of being analyzed and filtered in the natural state.

I have been asked frequently, "What if I don't dream?" If you go into unconscious sleep (delta brain wave) you have to go through the REM (rapid eye movement) state of consciousness (theta brain wave) which is where you dream but are not necessarily conscious of your dreams. Right before you awake you again enter or come up through the REM state and dream some more to vent out the unknown message units.

If you give yourself a suggestion right before going to sleep to—remember your venting dreams— you will begin to experience these dreams more and more. Sometimes they are bizarre and make no sense and occasionally they are quite pleasant and you'll want to go back to them.

Recurring dreams are fascinating and can hold a lot of useful information. Most hypnotherapists can help you to analyze these dreams. While there are several books on the subject about interpreting the symbols such as—what does a cow walking backwards mean? I have found that outside of general themes that may have some archetypical significance like deep water indicating deep or "scary" emotions, most of these symbols are only significant if they mean something to you. A good hypnotherapist can easily help you interpret the meanings in these dreams.

So, how much information (MU's) can the Critical mind hold before it "dumps" it all into the Subconscious mind? According to Dr. John Kappas, the subconscious portion of the Critical mind (the mind gate) can hold up to approximately twenty four hours of information before it has to release the information down into the Subconscious mind. The average time we are awake is sixteen hours so the Critical mind, under normal circumstances has roughly sixteen hours to analyze all this data before it is released down into the Subconscious mind when we go to sleep at night.

Overload/Overwhelmed
Causes fight/flight & Escape into hypnosis (flight)

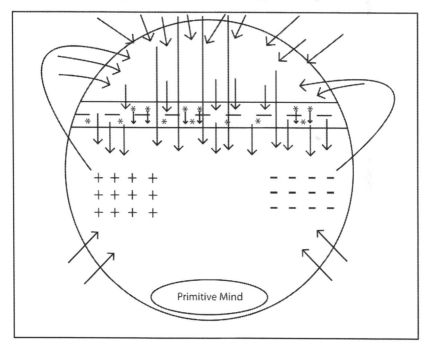

Fig. 5
Zone out.

Figure 5 demonstrates what happens when the Conscious mind becomes overloaded with information (MU's) coming from the environment, from other people, situations, circumstances and our own Subconscious mind which we interpret as thoughts. Our thoughts make up the bulk or majority of message units (MU's) that fill up the mind gate during the so-called waking state.

When we get too much information and become *overloaded* or overwhelmed— in the natural state (cave man days) we will just go to sleep. However, if we are unable to go to sleep (like when we are driving in commuter traffic) then we will go into a form of *simulated* sleep called a trance or hypnosis.

Just before this occurs, the sympathetic nervous system becomes stimulated and we may become a little nervous and jittery, as if we've had too much coffee. The Conscious mind perceives this *overload* as a potential threat which then triggers our fight or flight response! Now, if we can't fight— which often we cannot— especially if we are driving our car in commuter traffic or in the middle of an important meeting— we will escape (flight) into hypnosis (simulated sleep).

When we go into trance or hypnosis the brain becomes disorganized (the barrier breaks down) and all the information or message units (MU's) which would normally take about sixteen hours to analyze get downloaded into the Subconscious mind without being critically analyzed by our mind gate.

These message units can—and do— trigger programs in the Subconscious mind—creating even more message units— that bubble up into our Conscious mind. This constant influx of messages back into our Conscious mind keeps us in a state of overwhelm or overload for several hours or until we eventually fall asleep.

Exposure to too much stress— for too long a period of time—can keep us in a state of perpetual hypnosis. When we are in hypnosis, we become "hyper- suggestible". The term *hyper- suggestible* means we are easily persuaded, impressionable, gullible and susceptible— to outside influences because we are not filtering or blocking information (message units) from coming into our Conscious mind. The state of *hyper-suggestibility* is a term used by hypnotherapists to describe a *tranced* state. The client can *appear* to be wide awake but is not. Their Critical mind or *mind gate* is open and their gatekeeper is asleep at the wheel so— anything that may be going on in their environment— will go directly into their Subconscious mind and stimulate programs.

While hyper-suggestibility could be desirable when sitting in the hypnotherapist's chair and being given *positive suggestions* by the hypnotherapist—it is <u>not</u> a desirable condition if you're in the *waking* state and become hyper-suggestible during rush-hour traffic—or—if you take care of young children and any other time when it's crucial to keep your wits about you. It is very important and valuable to know how to stay out of hypnosis!

Going into hypnosis (hyper-suggestibility) can be dangerous because when the *Mind Gate* opens (becomes disorganized) during the waking state because there is a lot of information dropping into the Subconscious mind that has not been critically analyzed fully— the Conscious mind then becomes *confused*. Our behaviors can become somewhat erratic due to an inability to focus completely on <u>any </u>task at hand! Students who have difficulty with test-taking, even when they have studied and know the material tested, are almost always in a state of hypnosis or tranced.

The good news about this is—we have behavioral *patterns* that we have used over and over again for many years (like tying our shoes). We automatically go into these *automatic behavioral patterns* as a way of surviving overloads. For example— we may be driving down a road we've driven many times when we suddenly realize we missed our normal turnoff—and yet— we have been completely in control of the vehicle and still driving safely.

Emotional State/Tone

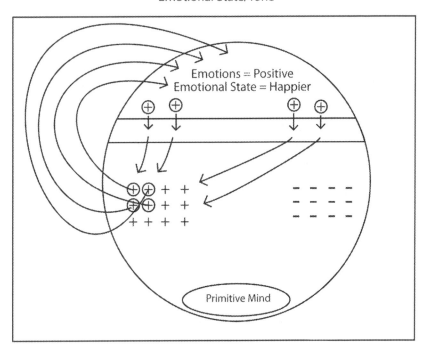

Fig. 6

Positive thoughts cause positive emotions.

One thing that is crucial to understanding how our mind works, is that our Subconscious *programming* is what creates our *emotional tones* or our *state-of-mind*! Notice in Fig.6 the positive programs (positive associations and identifications) are being stimulated. As these programs are stimulated they are sending or *uploading* message units into the Conscious mind in the form of thoughts. The body reacts to these *thought-forms* emotionally— in this case with good feelings. Then these good-feeling thoughts *create* more positive message units—that will eventually— be *dumped* or *dropped* into the Subconscious mind and stimulate even more positive programs.

Then the cycle repeats itself. This cycle is what creates our state of mind or emotional tone (how we feel). So, if you want to know what programs are being stimulated in the Subconscious mind— at any given moment— pay attention to how you feel!

Neuropsychologists estimate that over 70% of our Subconscious programming is *negative* so it would behoove us, a great deal— to care about how we *feel*.

Let's look again at the emotional tone scale and ask yourself how you are *feeling* right now.... after you've just read all the forgoing information. As you read through the list, one or more of these emotions will feel about right or you may just *feel* overwhelmed (Frustration).

Emotional Tone Scale

1. Joy—Empowerment—Freedom—Love—Appreciation
2. Passion for another—Passion
3. Enthusiasm—Eagerness—Happiness
4. Positive expectation—Positive beliefs
5. Optimism
6. Hopefulness
7. Contentment
8. Boredom
9. Pessimism
10. Frustration—Irritation—Impatience

11. Disappointment
12. Doubt
13. Worry
14. Blame
15. Discouragement
16. Anger
17. Revenge
18. Hatred—Rage
19. Jealousy
20. Insecurity—Guilt—Unworthy
21. Fear—Grief—Despair—Powerlessness

You don't have to go through the whole list on the emotional tone scale to *pinpoint* the emotion you are experiencing at any given time. Just notice if you feel *good* emotionally or *bad* emotionally! If you are *feeling* good— then try to keep thinking along the same lines as you have been thinking.

If you are feeling *bad* then quickly— or— as soon as possible— switch your thoughts to a little *better-feeling* thought!

It's a great idea to have a couple of *better-feeling* thoughts handy to help bring you up a few emotional notches when you need to. I have many of my clients write down as many good things as they can think of to use—as "emergency backups" until a full positive feedback loop can be established through repetition.

Remember, when we are in a hyper-suggestible state (hypnosis), we become confused— and it is more difficult to focus on anything! I have included a chapter on how to de-hypnotize our-self (Chapter 7: How to De-Hypnotize Ourselves) that discusses—in detail— how to recognize when you are in a state of hypnosis and then— how to get yourself out of the *tranced* or hypnotic state as soon as possible.

If you are not too far down on the *emotional tone scale* and you just want to feel better —it's easier to come up a little bit at a time by switching your thoughts to a little better-feeling thought! You can step it up a little more when you are able to get some alone time and do *the process*. The main thing here is to understand that *feeling* bad is usually a result of a negative programs running—and probably is not— what we think is happening— at all! Our perception is *faulty* when we are *tranced.*

Sometimes, this can be challenging, but remember, the Subconscious mind was programmed through— associations, identifications and repetition. It does have some *good* programs (known associations and identifications). It also has the capability of latching onto— an idea— if it is being fed that idea or picture repetitively. There are two laws at work here—the law of association and the law of repetition.

In order to *reprogram* the Subconscious mind so that it will be *bubbling* up a lot of positive thoughts to the Conscious mind— you will need to make it a habit — to regularly direct your attention to *good-feeling* thoughts!

The laws of repetition and association are your *keys* to all the *good stuff* you really want—along with the emotional tone scale!

I will discuss with you in detail how these laws work in *the Process*. The Subconscious mind can fixate for long periods of time on a central idea or thought— or thought pattern— if it is regularly stimulated (law of repetition).

Emotional State/Tone

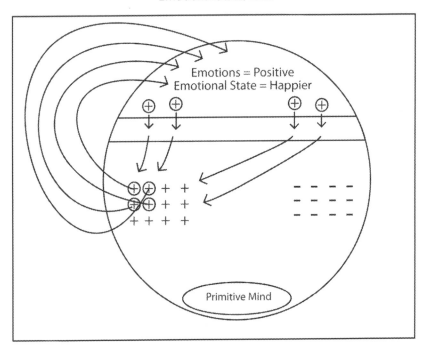

Fig. 6
Positive thoughts cause positive emotions.

Looking at figure 6 again.... notice that the *positive* thought patterns can be purposefully directed in the conscious state— and allowed clearance through the Mind Gate if— the idea is big enough—in other words, if the idea— has enough *energy* or *mass*.

Mass is achieved by using *imagery*—or—our imagination! Frequently clients tell me that they do not know how to visualize —but everyone can visualize but you can get a little rusty at it. If you can worry—you can visualize. I go over several techniques in Chapter 5: Imagination, to help you *remember* how to visualize.

Figure 6 represents what happens when the Subconscious mind is being stimulated by imagery from our Conscious mind— while in a conscious state.

There is a trick however to get through the Mind Gate and plant a positive idea and then to have it grow into a new positive program. You will learn this trick in Chapter 6: The Process.

As these new programs are stimulated or get switched-*on*— they are bubbling up…. sending up…. or uploading thoughts (or symbols which become thoughts) into our Conscious mind and then— the body responds with feelings or emotions!

Positive thought-forms that come from our Subconscious mind cause positive emotions— which in turn—create positive emotional states of mind (Fig.7-Positive Vibes). A positive emotional state *feels* good. By contrast, if negative programs are running in our Subconscious mind and they are being stimulated regularly, they are sending negative thought-forms up into our Conscious mind. These create negative emotional responses in the body and we *feel* bad. (Fig.8-Negative Vibes) Negative feelings or emotions create a *negative* state of mind!

A negative state of mind is like being in a bad mood and does not generally *feel* very good to us. So again, if you want to know which thoughts you have been thinking— or which programs are running and sending thoughts-forms into your Conscious mind—take a moment right now and just notice how you are *feeling.*

Are you feeling good or bad? If you are very ill, you probably have not been feeling too well emotionally either. You may have a *vague* sense of how you *feel* as you read these words.... or you may.... have a *strong* sense of how you are feeling—how do you feel most of the time?

Where on the emotional tone scale do you *hang-out* most of the time—or a lot of the time? More than likely, you hang-out in a fairly narrow range depending on several factors. When you are at work you may be very *different* emotionally than when you are at home or in certain social situations—or with certain groups of people. Start noticing more how you are *feeling* in these different areas of your life. If being around a certain person or persons feels bad, then that is your built-in guidance telling you something important.

If you are engaged in a favorite pastime or hobby you may feel *very different* emotionally than when you have to do—say—home maintenance.

The reason I am stressing this is because, as we become more aware of how we are feeling— we become more aware of what *programs* are being stimulated in our Subconscious mind!

These programs then—are creating energy— in the form of our *thoughts*— to enter into our Conscious mind— which then cause a corresponding emotion in our bodies!

These emotions cause even more message units ....or information in our Conscious mind that is about the *emotions* we are experiencing— which produces even more thoughts-forms, ad infinitum.

I want to be very clear about this. It's imperative— no, it is vital— that you understand—our moods are not coming from anything other than—our *programs*— that have been operating from our own Subconscious minds! This will really make sense to you when you begin to notice very soon that one day—you may be *feeling* good and then suddenly—for no reason— you may begin to *feel* bad.

Positive Vibes

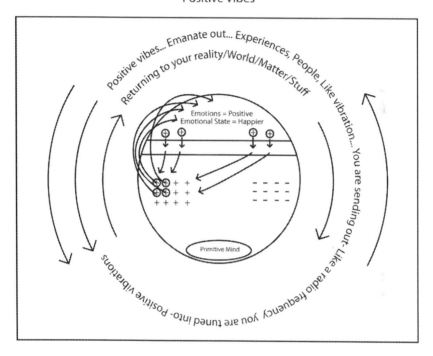

Fig. 7

Positive thoughts cause positive emotions.

Negative Vibes

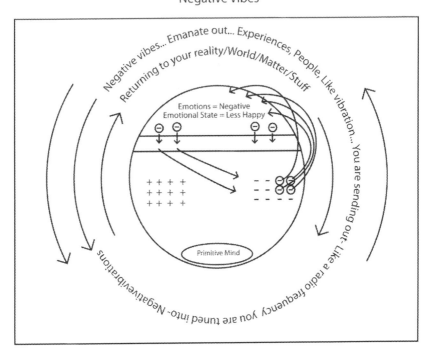

Fig. 8

Negative thoughts cause negative emotions.

Taking this to the next level, we can now see how we are attracting people— places—and things to us. And in so doing we are affecting the universe and the world…. the world we perceive! This is exactly how we manifest everything we experience in our world…and I do mean…. everything!

Figure 7 illustrates that the Subconscious minds positive *programs* are being stimulated by message units from the Conscious mind—which means— *you* have conscious control over what *programs* you want to be stimulated if you know how. The Mind Gate process I teach and developed helps you do just that!

Quantum physics experiments have demonstrated that— "Electrons (energy) in *wave* form are *forced* to behave as *particles*— when they are *observed* and, the greater amount of watching (observation) then the greater the observer's influence on what actually takes place ".-1998 Condensed Matter Physics Department, Israel.

What this means to you and I is this: as we observe or watch this energy- in- motion or (our moods and feelings) then the more we can control (literally) these emotions—to *make* them or *force* them to change to create what we want to experience! As we exercise our conscious control (on a regular basis) over our thoughts— we can directly influence exactly which of our Subconscious *programs* we want to stimulate!

In other words, by putting our *attention* on *positive* thoughts or ideas— our positive *programs* literally bubble up, send or upload more and more positive energy (thought-forms) into our Conscious mind. These *positive* thoughts *feel* good to us—creating even more *positive* message units. These positive message units (MU's) will then create even more *positive* or *good-feeling* thoughts that will be— dropped down— as positive message units into the *Mind Gate* for critical analysis. When we go to sleep or when we do *the process,* these positive message units will then be *downloaded* or dropped down into the Subconscious mind. *Positive* message units will stimulate even more of our *positive* programs that are already there in the Subconscious mind— or— create *new* positive programs. The *new* positive programs will then create even more *good-feeling* thoughts— producing even more message units that are positive which —well.... you get the message.

Our body's response to what scientists call waves of thought or *thought-forms* as they move up through the

Mind Gate to the Conscious mind could be called— *interference patterns* (Young's double-slit experiment in Chapter 8) when <u>un</u>*observed*— but when *observed* —can be molded or changed by what we *feel!*

Our emotions are quite literally energy-in-motion. They have an *observable* and *measurable* electromagnetic quality to them—and that energy— gets transmitted out from us and around us— and into the universe itself—just like a rock that has been thrown into quiet pond—known as *the ripple effect!*

Magnetoencephalograhy (MEG), is a *functional neuroimaging technique that can actually map our brain's activity by recording magnetic fields* produced by electrical currents occurring naturally in our brains. Here's the corker....theses magnetic fields are recorded *outside* of our heads! How can this be?

The research being conducted with the use of MEG, in my opinion, is irrefutable scientific proof that our brain's activity (including our thoughts and emotions) is not limited to the body as commonly believed. Could it be that MEG is demonstrating to us that we are indeed signaling or communicating to others and the universe with some bio-radio wave?

Positive Vibes

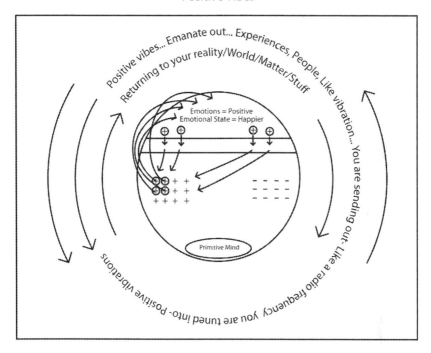

Fig. 7

Positive thoughts cause positive emotions.

Negative Vibes

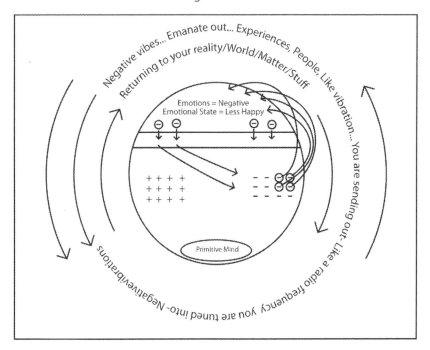

Fig. 8
Negative thoughts cause negative emotions.

In contrast to figure 7, when you look at figure 8 you will notice that the *negative programs* are being stimulated from *thinking* negative thoughts. These negative thoughts are dumping negative message units (MU's) into the Subconscious mind!

When these negative programs are turned on.... they bubble up, send or upload *negative* thoughts-forms into the Conscious mind— which in turn—creates a negative body response (bad-feeling emotion).

This is a great time to *observe* these emotions or feelings! Negative emotions such as Disappointment, Doubt, Worry,

Blame, Discouragement, Anger, Revenge, Hatred, Jealousy, Guilt, Fear, and Grief will be felt in the body some place. A good exercise is to try and locate what part of the body is *feeling* the negative emotion the most.

Is it in your heart, your head, your stomach, solar plexus, back or neck? The flip-side of this may be—when you are feeling discomfort in some part of your body, take a few moments and see if you can identify the emotion on *the emotional tone scale* that corresponds to the discomfort.

For example—pain in the middle or upper back can be connected to the emotion of Guilt.

> "All that stuff that is in back of us. Are you afraid
> to see what is back there, or are you hiding what
> is back there? Do you feel stabbed in the back?"—
> from "You Can Heal Your Life" by Louise L. Hay

Going to sleep when any of these feelings are going strong means the *program* that created those feelings will become a little easier to stimulate the next time.

There's an old Adage about having a happy marriage that I always thought was very good advice. It goes like this. *Never go to bed angry with each other.* That, in my opinion is great advice whether you are living with a partner or not. I would take that a step further and advise you to never go to bed with negative emotions of any kind, and especially, never go to bed being angry with yourself.

Watching the news, reading the news, watching *negative* shows or movies or even reading a book with *negative* themes can stimulate negative programs. I'm just saying—be vigilant and be aware! Dr. John Kappas used to talk quite a bit about what he called "the Magic thirty minutes." He was talking about the last thirty minutes before sleep—suggestions, thoughts or emotions (and especially visualizations or imaginings) will be at their *most powerful*.... so be very aware of how you are *feeling* before falling asleep!

If you have children—whenever possible—don't let them go to bed with negative emotions. Bedtime is not a good time to punish children If you are feeling any negative feelings on a regular basis during waking hours— and haven't observed the feelings—but prefer to ignore them or *stuff them*—then you will be sending these *stuffed* feeling message units back into the Subconscious mind anyway when you go to sleep, so learn how to process them as soon as possible by observing them. Then you can turn your attention to something more positive. Jesus gave us some great advice when he said to "....turn the other cheek...."

For example: If you are going to sleep worrying about the bills and how you are going to pay them.....acknowledge that you feel you are in a jam....to yourself! Then ask that your higher (or a higher) power take on the burden of your bills— and then thank this higher power—sincerely. Better yet, write it down before going to sleep. (See Chapter 4: Mastering the Emotional Tone Scale and read The God List). Then you can go to sleep feeling better because you got the worries out of your head and down on paper. This sends a strong message to your Subconscious mind that—all is well!

Even if you decide not to deal with your negative emotions and keep stuffing them down, where do you think you've stuffed them? They are either in your body or already in the Subconscious mind. They may have already started some negative momentum of their own and may already be showing up as negative thoughts. They can develop a lot of energy if they have been occupying your thoughts all day and probably have already been *dropped* into the Subconscious mind when you *zoned-out* from the stress of it all.

Remember, before you go to sleep at night and again upon awakening in the morning you go through the brain wave state of hypnosis. You'll want to get rid of or at least try to displace any negative feelings you may be feeling as soon as possible—because—you are traveling through the *Mind Gate* at those times when you naturally go into and come out of hypnosis. The bigger the emotions you may be feeling, the stronger the *suggestion* will be to the Subconscious mind—and—the more energy that will be put out into the universe or *field*. So, you will want as much *good-feeling* stuff going on (emotionally) as you possibly can before sleep and when you wake up.

Human Radio Transmitter

I'll give you a wonderful technique for clearing the day's negative emotions before sleep so less negative energy gets down into your Subconscious programs in Chapter 4: Mastering the Emotional Tone Scale-Unwinding Negative Energy. The good news is this. Good feelings on the higher levels of the emotional tone scale like Joy— Freedom— Love— Appreciation and Passion carry a bigger emotional charge than the lower tones with the exception of Anger and therefore— create more energy as they drop into the Subconscious mind. But never underestimate the intense emotions at the lower end of the tone scale like Fear. Do you remember "the dark side" from Star Wars?

Fear is so rampant in our societies that it can send out a very strong signal. I will give you techniques to *interrupt* these negative patterns so you will stop creating negative experiences for your-self and others. You can think of these signals as images that bounce off mirrors in the world and are reflected back to you or you can think of them as radio waves or signals to the universal energy field that comes back to you in like experiences. Any way you want to think of it will work just fine just so long as you understand that it is YOU that are doing all the *creating* here, whether intentionally or by default.

The stronger the emotion— the bigger the mass and energy and— the faster the momentum—so learn how to observe those emotions as energy-in-motion and then— learn how to control them. Remember my Fear of the snowstorm and the mountain highway the night of my car accident?

Do you know what you have been transmitting out to the universal energy field? What do you *want* to be transmitting out into the Universe? Once a negative or positive program gets going (attention put on it) it develops momentum so *like* thoughts create *like* emotions and then *like* emotions send out *like feelings* into the universal energy field much like a radio transmitter or sonar device. Then, *like* physical matter and energy shows up in our physical time-space reality. As we notice our physical reality, we have thoughts and feelings about it which then create more similar or *like* message units.

And *like* message units (MU's) stimulate *like* Subconscious *knowns* or programs and.... did I cover this already?

These emotions of ours have energy because they are, quite literally, *energy in motion*. They are sending out signals throughout the universe like a powerful radio tower or like ripples in a still pond when a pebble is dropped into it. They have an effect on the universe— the entire universe. It becomes imperative then, to learn about and then *master* your emotions!

CHAPTER 4

Mastering the Emotional Tone Scale

"See no evil, Hear no evil,
Speak no evil, Do no evil"
—an ancient Japanese proverb

It will assist you greatly to take a few moments and write down any stories from your past that may live in your memory as important or significant times in your history. After you jot down your memoirs, see if you can identify the emotional tones you were experiencing during or around that time. If you do this sincerely, you will discover the *why* of your behaviors back then. You may even get an "aha" moment that will be a wonderful validation for your past responses.

As an example, I'd like you to remember my story from Chapter 2: The Cloak Room (State of Joy). I'll refresh your memory. My emotional tone or state of mind went from Insecurity (when I printed my letters backward) which *made me* behave in a way that attracted the Anger of my teacher (I was disturbing other students in the classroom). Her Anger moved her to *march* me to the cloak room in the back of the first grade school building and made me sit on the floor there—away from the rest of the class. As I was sitting in the cloakroom *feeling* Guilty, I noticed the door to outside the school building was ajar. I began having thoughts about leaving the building. I then began *picturing* in my mind how being *outside* would *feel*. Then, even more thoughts of how it would *feel* being *outside* came into my conscious awareness.

As more of these *good-feeling* or *positive* thoughts were coming to me, I began feeling better and better and my emotional tone began— rising like a cork released— and bobbing toward the surface of a pond after being held under water. As my state of mind rose—to a higher tone of Freedom, I had no choice except to get up from the floor and walk out the door to— Freedom! Just like Peter Pan, I could fly— with my happy thoughts. Take a look at the emotional tone scale again.

Emotional Tone Scale

1. Joy—Empowerment—Freedom—Love— Appreciation
2. Passion for another—Passion
3. Enthusiasm—Eagerness—Happiness
4. Positive expectation—Positive beliefs
5. Optimism
6. Hopefulness
7. Contentment
8. Boredom
9. Pessimism
10. Frustration—Irritation—Impatience
11. Disappointment
12. Doubt

13. Worry
14. Blame
15. Discouragement
16. Anger
17. Revenge
18. Hatred—Rage
19. Jealousy
20. Insecurity—Guilt—Unworthy
21. Fear—Grief—Despair—Powerlessness

Now— think back to my other story from Chapter 2-The Diagnosis (State of Fear). I had become so overwhelmed or *overloaded* with MU's (message units) daily when starting a chiropractic practice on my own— with all the responsibilities, debt and burden of the business resting squarely on my shoulders. Prior to starting my practice I had been *overloaded* from taking National and State Board exams. Prior to that for at least four years I was often in a state of— *overload*— from the intensity of professional college and before that— pre-med studies.

In addition, I held down a job and worked all through my college years and had even gone through a divorce while still in Chiropractic College. All the while, maintaining my grades, doing my internship and preparing for the National and State Board exams. In short, I was in a state of *overload* a lot and— for many, many years. But, with school breaks, rest and a Hopeful state of mind— I always bounced back to an emotional tone of Positive Expectation.

Do you remember what happens when we become overwhelmed or overloaded? That's right, we go into hypnosis. When we are in hypnosis we become *hyper-suggestible*. When we are walking around in a state of hyper-suggestibility and are exposed to massive amounts of information coming into our Conscious mind—all that information gets *dumped* into our Subconscious mind without being analyzed by our critical mind.

The mind gate is open, letting all of this information or message units pour into our Subconscious mind stimulating programs— that are *like* those message units. If we are subjected to a lot of *negative* information, we are more likely to have *negative* thoughts uploaded to our Conscious mind that are in the lower end of the emotional tone scale.

As a result of being in hypnosis for extended periods of time, my Fear programs, and Insecurity programs were getting stimulated frequently. So, when I began feeling the pain in my lower stomach, which in and of itself created huge amounts of information or message units coming from my body hourly— more and more of my negative (Fear) programs were getting stimulated.

Because of my training in diagnosis, I was also trying to *figure* out what was causing the pain— I was thinking a lot about it, especially at night before sleep and also first thing in the morning when I woke up—becoming obsessed. The more I felt the pain— the more I thought about it—the more I thought about it— the more I felt Worry and Fear.

Remember, we naturally go into hypnosis when we go to sleep and again when we wake up so, these are not good times to be thinking or talking *negatively* to our-selves. Of course, there is no *good time* to be talking *negatively* to our-self— but especially— not those two times.

Having very limited knowledge of the Critical mind (*mind gate*) at that time— and having only basic education from psychology and psychiatry classes about the workings of the Conscious and Subconscious minds—I did nothing to close the *mind gate* to protect myself from the vicious cycle and negative momentum—that had already started. I knew nothing about the *law of attraction* and only had a cursory understanding of the emotional tone scale and— I was compounding this negative situation daily by trying to diagnose all my symptoms— myself! And all the while, I was giving myself even more negative suggestions.

Finally, my pain had increased to a point where I could no longer ignore it. I went to a colleague to get an x-ray of my lower back and pelvis. At this point I was even in a more continual state of *overload* or *trance.*

To say I was hyper-suggestible is an understatement. When I viewed the x-rays my colleague had taken of my lower back and pelvis and saw— this obvious *abnormality* in my pelvic bone, I sank quickly— into the emotional tone of Fear. I was trying desperately to get a handle on my Fear but— like a dog that has fallen into a deep well and keeps pawing at the stone to get a foothold— all the while treading water and getting weaker by the minute—I had fallen into an emotional abyss. My breath came faster as my heart pounded-ever harder in my head— I was trying to *fight- off* panic. I was trying desperately to climb up the emotional tone scale toward Hopefulness but— I was way too deep in hypnosis and too far down the scale to make the jump from Fear to Hopefulness.

The stresses of my life's situations for the last several years had served to put me— in and out— of hypnosis where I had not been *mindful* of my state of mind and had not been vigilant enough to guard against negativity very well. With a great amount of mental effort, I was able to come up the scale to Worry. But I soon plummeted back down to Fear after speaking to my colleague's associate about my x-ray findings. The *negative* message units continued until I became stuck

in the emotional tone of Fear. Fear and dread became my constant companions for the next year. Sometimes I would wake up feeling refreshed and for a moment thinking that this was all just— a bad dream but then the pain would *stab* and *jab* me back into my dark *reality.*
During the day, when I was working with my own patients, I would be distracted enough to get a little relief from my thoughts and feelings of Fear and Despair. One day bled over into the next as I muddled through a grim reality that had me *overloaded* on a daily basis. Several months later, after being on an emotional roller coaster between Anger and Despair— mostly Despair, my state of mind had *leveled-off* a little and had risen up to the emotional tone level of Irritation and Impatience. Remember these tones are higher than Fear and Despair. The Irritation continued long enough for me to make the decision to go forward and get a biopsy. I needed to find out once and for all if "the thing" in my pelvis was malignant or not.

I said in my story that I finally rose to the level of Courage or Irritation and Impatience to face the Fear. At least, that is how I thought of it at the time and still do. It does indeed take Courage to be hopeful in the face of hopelessness, but I was nowhere near the emotional tone of Hopeful. I was actually becoming "pissed off"! In other words, I had reached the emotional tone of Anger and Anger gets things moving.

Reflecting back on that time, I believe that I was getting Irritated and Impatient with my body and its continual reminders of my immortality. Eventually, the Irritation drove me down into the emotional tone of Anger. Anger is a very, very powerful emotion and can serve us well— if used correctly. When I'd found out, following the biopsy that the tumor (or whatever it was) was not malignant, I felt a huge release of negative emotions. I then bounced up the emotional tone scale even higher—all the way up to Optimism.

Within a few weeks I received the happy news from orthopedic surgeon number two in the form of a letter that matched my emotional tone of Optimism— exactly. The results from the surgical removal confirmed that the "osteochondroma" was indeed— benign.

My emotional tone rose once again, now to Positive Expectation and I felt like now, I could finally get on with my life. I know, in my *heart of hearts*, that my Optimistic state of mind and the sometimes higher tone of Positive Expectation and Beliefs definitely affected the outcome. And— I really want you to hear this—while recovering from my surgery, colleagues and friends came to my office in the evenings, after they had finished with their own patients and took care of my patients. They did not take any money for their services.

This would not be the last time I would be in a similar need. The happy outcome and healing— from an illness and life situation, that from all earlier appearances looked as if it would end in my suffering and death—I attribute solely to the radical shift in my emotional tone.

Emotional Tone Scale

1. Joy—Empowerment—Freedom—Love— Appreciation
2. Passion for another—Passion
3. Enthusiasm—Eagerness—Happiness
4. Positive expectation—Positive beliefs
5. Optimism
6. Hopefulness

7. Contentment
8. Boredom
9. Pessimism
10. Frustration—Irritation—Impatience
11. Disappointment
12. Doubt
13. Worry
14. Blame
15. Discouragement
16. Anger
17. Revenge
18. Hatred-rage
19. Jealousy
20. Insecurity—Guilt—Unworthy
21. Fear—Grief—Despair—Powerlessness

The Emergency Brake

To master the emotional tone scale you first have to understand that— you actually can! This technique has to be *practiced* to build up enough energy in reserve to not be thrown off balance when a momentum of lower tone energy comes our way— which it will for a while. For example— you may be thinking about all the bills you owe and how each month there is *not enough money* to pay them all. To stop the negative momentum of *not enough money* you will need to halt— or at least— slow down this momentum as soon as possible. How can we do this?

We need to employ *The Emergency Brake* at the first indicator or sign that we are going down the scale emotionally— in other words— when we begin to *feel* bad. Unfortunately, we usually wait until we *feel* bad physically before we even have any awareness that there is a problem. Do you remember how I went into denial in order to deal with the other part of my life after receiving what I *perceived* as a diagnosis of a malignancy?

Let's say your state of mind (your mood or emotional tone) this morning was Worry—and— as the day wore on you began to have *feelings* of Fear or Grief. That's when you need to realize that your emotional tone has nose-dived and *emergency action* is required.

Take a moment by yourself (take a bathroom break if you are at work) and breathe deep into the belly. Standing up is preferable here. As you take— five deep breaths into the belly— exhaling a little more slowly than you breathe in— *call up* or *feel* some Anger about these Fear *programs* that are running. Raise your Anger up higher now about these programs trying to ruin your state of mind. Be clear that, even if there may be a vague reason for the Fear, if there's no eminent danger present then—go ahead— get *pissed off*. Direct the Anger at the *programs* that are causing the negative emotions you are feeling. Feel the Anger some more and as it becomes more intense— direct it toward the negative programs (Fear or Grief). If you can shout out loud, say something like— "Get off my back... get off my back" and move as if you are throwing an unwanted guest off your back or— if you simply scream loudly (or loudly to yourself), "No, No, No!" or "No More, No More, No More, You are just a program and I will not let you Ruin My Life!". Whatever feels the most powerful to you is what you want to use.

Clinch your fist if you have to and shake as you *feel* the Anger building in your body. Do this as many times as it takes or however many days it takes. Each time you do this— take a few moments and *observe* any negative thoughts or feelings that may still be hanging around. The idea here is to move emotional energy off the lower tones. From Anger, you can usually *feel* your way up to the higher tones of Frustration—Irritation—Impatience fairly easily. I have used this technique to move me off Worry and Discouragement even though they are higher up on the scale than Anger. Feel the Anger as it *snaps* you out of the abyss and lands you up the scale somewhere else— then let it go!

If you are gripped with Fearful or Guilty thoughts and there is no immediate or eminent threat to your life or you haven't done anything to feel guilty about— that is solid *evidence* that there is a program running away with your mind. That's a good time to use The Emergency Brake. This technique works because Anger is a very powerful emotion. We have this emotion to protect us or our loved ones— and to put in our boundaries (see Chapter 9: Channeled, and read *I Am*).

Remember, you will be directing your Anger only at the negative programs—never at another person—especially yourself! This serves two purposes:

1.) You will not be hurting yourself or anyone else and
2.) This is a powerful affirmation that you have control over your emotions while also affirming the thoughts that create the negative emotions are indeed, just programs that are running.

When you are operating or hanging-out frequently on a level (emotional tone) between Guilt and Fear—you are treading on very thin ice my friend, and I would advise you to go after those *negative* programs as soon as possible.

Remember The Emergency Brake technique and use Anger or any other tone that will help you snap-out of those lower tones and programs quickly. I know That some of you may have *programs* that may be wired up something like this: *it's a sin to feel or be angry*—but I can assure you—there is no sin in protecting yourself and others from the harm that can come from being in Fear.

Mat Work

I learned this technique over twenty years ago at "Shalom" retreats and workshops from an amazing teacher and psychotherapist by the name of Charles "Charlie" Lindberg. It was a very powerful and transformational experience to kick and scream on "the Mat" (a mattress) releasing *tons* of blocked emotional energy to move you on up the emotional tone scale. You may have guessed already that a lot of Grief can be released by using the emotional tone of Anger.

While the Shalom process was a powerful, experiential process, you don't always need an entire three-day workshop to be able to move the negative emotional energies. It can be just as effective (or even more) to daily do something to move the negative energy out of your body. But, if you feel you need to be *snapped* into reality, then Shalom workshops or other types of these processes may be exactly what you need.

You can derive great benefit by taking a tennis racket and then *whack* it against a vinyl- covered cushion— making an amazing sound. If you do this and shout "NO, NO, NO…." at the same time— it is particularly effective— to move the emotional energy up the scale. This makes us *feel* empowered and again, utilizes the emotional tone of Anger to move the energy up the scale.

Fear is extremely dis-empowering so, any emotion above Fear is a step up. A word of caution here would be to always remember that calling upon this powerful emotional tone of Anger, while a powerful tool is like fire— it can burn you— and others— badly. So, always direct Anger at the negative programs— and never—at other people, animals or things. And never, ever —direct it at yourself!

The God List

One of the most powerful processes I've ever used to move negative energy fast is what I call— The God List. This could also be called— the Higher Power List— the Universe List or My Higher-Self List, if you'd like. It doesn't matter what you call it just as long as you have some *belief* that there exist—a power somewhere—that knows a lot more than your own Conscious mind. If you think of this power as the same power that suspends the planets in their orbits you'd have to admit that is a pretty powerful energy or force. Hmmm....that might be a good name for it—how about—The Force List?

> "Truly I tell you, if you have faith as small as a mustard seed, you can say to this mountain, 'Move from here to there,' and it will move. Nothing will be impossible for you"-Matthew 17:20

Anyway, here's how it works. Anything that is occupying *space* in your Conscious mind as a worry or concern affects the natural flow of good into your life—so take a sheet of paper and draw a line down the middle. On the left write the word "me" in lower case letters, indicating less intelligence and powerlessness. On the right side write or print the word GOD, UNIVERSE, HIGHER-SELF or THE FORCE in upper case letters, indicating unlimited intelligence and power.

Then under "me" write one, two or three things you can do today! This can be as simple as "eat healthy" or "give the dog a bath" or "call the power company", etc.

On the right side—under THE FORCE (or whatever you prefer) write anything that worries you, such as "money to pay the rent" or "my low back pain" or "conflict with my child, spouse, boss", etc.

The point is this—by writing down the worry or concern you are using your Subconscious mind. Writing is what hypnotherapist and handwriting experts call an *ideomotor response*. An *ideomotor* response is something we have practiced over and over like tying our shoes and involves very little conscious effort, which means it comes largely from the Subconscious. This sends a very powerful message to your Subconscious mind that you are turning over these concerns to a higher power so it can stop *bubbling* up negative messages into our Conscious mind about the concern.

You will be amazed how fast this works. This also works beautifully on goals you want to achieve or literally anything you want handled. The idea here is to get your monkey mind to stop its incessant chatter and let the higher Source deal with it. You don't need to figure it all out in your Conscious mind. In fact, trying to *figure out* how you are going to pay the rent or score a great new job or relationship is futile. It only invites more torture from your *monkey mind*. In Alcoholics Anonymous circles there is a wise saying—*Our best thinking got us here.*

This technique, when combined with visualization is so powerful for creating change and achieving our goals that I could write a book just about these two processes— and I might do just that!

Unwinding Negative Energy

This is a technique to get rid of negative energy you may have accumulated throughout the day. Remember to never go to sleep with a lot of negative emotions or in negative surroundings whenever possible because, they can activate negative programs in the subconscious. This can often cause horrible nightmares that can affect your state of mind negatively for days or even longer.

If you are experiencing negative feelings before bed— try this. It's an ancient technique and reportedly was used by the Buddha quite a lot. Right before sleep, breathe deeply into the abdomen for five minutes and then imagine or pretend that you are going through your day— in reverse.

See yourself putting on your night clothes— then brushing your teeth, taking off your makeup, taking off your day clothes, eating dinner and so on—all the way back to waking up to start your day.

You start from where you are and go backward through the day—step by step until you see and *feel* yourself in the bed when you last woke up. With each remembered *encounter* with any type of negativity whatsoever— you must remind yourself—you are only watching a movie or *observing* the emotional responses you may have experienced and then try to see this as—a learning experience.

For example—if someone was rude and angry, even if it was not directed at you, perhaps your body responded with Fear, rather than feeling that Fear again,(which would actually be doing violence to yourself) remind yourself that you are doing this exercise to be the *observer,* so you may want to think; "I attracted that mirror to show me I need to raise my emotional tone so that I don't attract any more of those experiences." This is a great exercise to see these negative programs for what they really are—just programs!

This technique will *literally* throw off negative emotional energy by the *bucketful* and, your Subconscious mind won't be stimulated nearly as much. You will sleep much better and you will have a much better chance of waking up in a better state of mind. It's important to remember that energy (and you) are never static and are always moving. You just want it to be moving in the right direction.

Pleasure and Pain—Upgrades

We need to set aside at least ten to fifteen minutes a day when we will not be disturbed so we can *get in touch* with our energy. If we have some lower tone emotions that may have already developed some significant momentum (you are becoming aware of the physical manifestation of those feelings in your physical reality) then we must work on those negative emotions first. For example—if you have a negative life situation continuing, such as being overweight, you must first understand that you have *thoughts* and *feelings* about the situation. If you are *overweight* and have tried various diets— and your body seems to be resisting losing the weight—and this is disturbing to you every time you look in the mirror, then, you can be fairly sure that the situation has a lot of momentum going.

Anything that has already *manifested* in your world, including being overweight, has had a lot of mental energy (thoughts about it) and emotion (your body's response to those thoughts) put into it until—it eventually manifested. In other words, the momentum of these negative programs is going too fast to stop now (like a run-away train) because they have already manifested in your physical world.... Bummer!

Many of these—hopefully—are just a matter of preference, like; you'd prefer a better work situation or you'd like to lose ten pounds. If how you are feeling about it is above the emotional tones of Frustration—Irritation— Impatience on the emotional tone scale, then you can use *the process* to create a preferred work situation or easily lose the ten pounds, more or less, at your leisure. However, if you *check out* your feelings on the emotional tone scale about any situation that resonates at Revenge or lower then, you must apply The Emergency Brake method to move that energy back up the scale—as soon as possible.

Other unpleasant manifestations that have less *emotional intensity* around them need to be addressed eventually, but I would suggest that first, in the case of being overweight, write down on a notepad what you *like* about being overweight. I understand that you may not believe you like anything about being overweight—and consciously—I'm sure there may not be anything you like about being overweight but, *subconsciously* ....you do!

Remember that our subconscious *programs* came from our (known) associations and identifications and these known associations and identifications represent *pleasure* to our Subconscious mind and *unknown* information represents *pain to* our Subconscious *programs*. For instance—eating high calorie food could represent *pleasure* and exercise could represent *pain* to your Subconscious mind.

So, if you are overweight and are not consciously *okay* about it, then you have a program in your Subconscious mind that is running and— it is getting enough attention and energy to keep it running. In other words, it keeps getting stimulated by thoughts and feelings you are having about it!

Now, look into a mirror at your naked body and say to yourself (or better yet, out loud) "Look what I created!" This will remind you that you have *power* over this situation, because— if you created it then you must be able to— stop creating it! And then, look into your eyes in the mirror, and ask yourself— "How do I *feel* about (this situation)?"

What will surface will be an *emotional* answer or *tone* that you'll be able to peg somewhere on the emotional tone scale. At the very least, you will *feel* bad or you will *feel* good. Of course, there is always the third possibility that you will feel neutral. If you feel neutral about your issue(s) then take that as a— *feel* good!

When you are able to peg an emotion, for instance — Frustration—then look at the emotional tone scale again and look to see what the next tone up is which is Pessimism. While it may *not* be where you eventually want to be emotionally on the scale in regards to your weight it is still a higher tone than Frustration so it will *feel* a little better to you.

It's okay to feel Pessimistic about your weight, especially if you've been hanging-out in a lower tone about this issue for a long time. Or, maybe you feel Despair over your weight. Any tone up the scale will be an improvement, so maybe you could get Angry about the situation…. not Angry at yourself .... just Angry about the life situation your *programs* have created for you.

Somehow and some way— you must get your energy moving up the scale. Emotions are quite literally energy-in-motion so you need to be working on changing your thoughts about any *life situation* you may be challenged with. Even if, it means, calling up your Anger. You could go into the woods or an abandoned building and scream, if you need to, just as long as you direct your Anger at the *programs* and not anyone or anything else. It is okay to direct your Anger at the situation, as long as you remember, it is just a program you are using to deal with another program. Some people have subconscious programs that make them too thin to the detriment of their health.

Perhaps you could think of the emotional tone scale like a video game. When you've mastered one level then you can move up to the next level. Once you're able to feel Hopeful in regards to any issue or life situation then you will make rapid progress from there. The tone of Hopeful is like being in a hot air balloon with the anchors dropped and the burners at full flame. You'll rise easily up from there—so Hopeful is a great emotional goal to reach for.

When you practice *The Mind Gate Process of Empowerment*, you may not be able to jump all the way up the scale to *Joy* at first. But, if you have to climb up one rung of the emotional tone scale ladder at a time.... that is perfectly okay. In fact, it is the only way you reach the upper tones— although you may never become aware of the rungs as you climb the emotional tone *ladder*. This is how all the masters have learned how to manage their states.

What *thought* do you think—would bring you up a *rung* or two on the emotional tone scale? That's the thought you will need to be thinking for a while about— any particular subject or life situation— to shift the energy. When you can wrap your head around the emotional tone scale and realize that emotions are just your body responding to your so-called *thoughts* (subconscious programs) you will *master* your mind.

Negative programs that have gained enough momentum to manifest are like runaway trains and the only way to put on the brakes and slow them down is to consciously think a better- feeling thought about the situation (see Reframes in Chapter 4). However, once they have actually become manifest (appear in your life) you cannot really *un-manifest* them but— you can take *your attention* away from them by focusing on what you really want instead. This is the meaning of what Jesus said by "….turn the other cheek". You can do this in a number of ways and I will discuss some of those with you, but by far the fastest and the most effective way is by enlisting your *imagination*.

Vision Boards & Mind Movies

There are many tools to stimulate your imagination and help you to move up the emotional tone scale to Joy—but few are as powerful as—Vision Boards. A vision board is simply a *collage* of pictures that represent some thing or situation that makes you feel positive emotion when you imagine having it as a reality in your life. These pictures or visual images could be taped or pasted on a poster board; thumb tacked on a corkboard or even plastered all over a wall. They just need to be someplace where you can see them—all together ideally. If you'd like— you can have more than one— or with today's technology— you can even have a collage on your smartphone or computer screen as wallpaper.

Here are the tricks to vision boards— the pictures need to be something that means something *very special* to you— not someone else. It will be important and necessary to spend a little time each day—looking and daydreaming— about them. Five to ten minutes is sufficient. If the pictures are tied into your daily meditation and visualization in some way then your *vision board* will be infinitely more powerful.

I remember when I first heard about *vision boards*. It was back in the early 1980's— and pictures of what I wanted got put on the refrigerator. These pictures can be a *symbol* of what you want and not necessarily the exact item or circumstance— for instance— a Rolls Royce parked in the driveway of a mansion —if you want to be a millionaire— could represent more than enough financial wealth. But be careful because, your *monkey mind* may use it against you. What I call the *monkey mind* is all the mental noise or *chatter* that is going on— most of the time that we are only vaguely aware of as a constant stream of consciousness or *thought- stream*.

The *monkey mind* is the *conscious* part of our Critical mind (mind gate) that is incessantly analyzing the message units that have been dropped into it from all sources, including the Subconscious programs that have *bubbled* up as our so-called thoughts. The picture of the Rolls Royce for example, may be so far out of our Subconscious mind's positive programing that it stimulates negative programs that might be *wired* something like this— "I always have to struggle to make a living" or "Rich people are all crooks". So, a little word of caution is in order here.

If the pictures on your vision board don't make you *feel* good when you imagine the reality the picture points to, you could unwittingly be stimulating some of your negative programs. This can make you feel like you are paddling upstream or against the current and struggling unnecessarily.

One of my favorite sayings that my mother-in-law Joyce used to say, following a wildly positive statement—made by her or someone else was, "It could happen!"

If the image of taking a cruise to the Bahamas still *feels* good when you imagine it saying to yourself, "It could happen!" then it is probably a go. Keep in mind that the real value here will be in reaching for— and then attaining a higher emotional tone. If you are *stressing* over an event or are *addicted* to a *specific outcome*— or a nearly *unattainable* goal you may be sabotaging yourself and — creating even more resistance— which could actually drive your emotional tone down into Frustration or worse.

When I say *unattainable* goal, I am referring to an obvious difficulty that is unlikely to result in the feelings you want. For example— I used to dream of being an astronaut. I just loved the idea of space flight since I was a small child. Then, on February 20, 1962— John Glenn became the first man to orbit the earth. He orbited the earth three times and reached speeds of 17,000 miles per hour! My dreams had just gotten closer to— someday— becoming a reality for me. Although now, I would still love to fly into space, I most likely couldn't qualify to be an astronaut— at this time but, I may have a chance to fly into space as a passenger someday— "It could happen!"

It bears repeating here that it is not absolutely necessary to know, exactly what it is that you want. When it comes right down to it, you may only want the *feeling* of having something, like a Rolls Royce or space flight. As you look at the picture of the Rolls, focus on how that might *feel* to be driving down the road in a Rolls Royce Corniche convertible with the wind blowing through your hair— the smell of rich leather interior— the feel of the road melting under the car as you listen to its quadraphonic sound system playing your favorite tunes. If you don't have to have a Rolls Royce but enjoy the fantasy as you look at the picture then that is still extremely valuable to you because, who knows all the good— that *feeling* —will do for you.

So again, you may want to go general here with pictures of beautiful scenery like a beautiful sunset, a tropical beach or a mountain meadow. Personally, I've always liked the idea of the Rolls Royce Corniche since I saw the movie "10" with Dudley Moore. Any picture that represents the emotional tone of Joy to you is very, very good. Laughing babies or a bunch of helium-filled balloons rising toward the sky, a Rolls Royce or Space Craft are all wonderful (I have a picture of the starship, USS Enterprise tacked on my vision board—I haven't given up yet). It's perfectly okay to use any and all pictures you want as long as the pictures *feel* good when you look at them. You'll want to spend at least about five minutes a day looking at them but ten minutes is better. It speeds things along to fantasize about them becoming or being a reality in your life so—have fun!

Again— in the morning and before bed are ideal times. If you Google *vision boards* there are a few websites that will give you lots of good ideas. In the 1980's when AMWAY was going strong in our town, my waiting room magazines suffered terribly. Fortunately, we no longer have to go through magazines and cut out pictures because there are tons of images you can download and print from Google Images on just about any subject you could think of.

I love "Laughing Babies" from Google images or even better, "Laughing Babies" on YouTube—talk about belly-laughs— OMG, these will kick you right up the emotional tone scale to at least—the tone of Optimism. Watch these for at least five minutes. The point is that you need to look at pictures that make you feel really good in order to raise *your* emotional tone.

A new twist on the vision boards, are "Mind-Movies". Basically— they are a power point collage with pictures, positive affirmations and inspiring music that can all be custom-made for you. It's a great idea— but as always— check these with your internal *emotional guidance* (how do they feel to you?) before you choose the pictures and affirmations.

They must *feel* good to you and not trigger negative subconscious programming. I'm not too sure about pre-made videos because— this is your Subconscious mind we are talking about. But, as long as they check out okay (feel good) with your *emotional guidance* and you *feel* positive emotions when watching them— they are good. You only want to let what *feels* good to you—go through the Mind Gate. That said, a Mind Movie could be a very powerful tool— especially a customized one when used in conjunction with *the process.*

AFFIRMATIONS AND REFRAMING

Affirmations are positive statements or suggestions given to ourselves. In other words, they are "positive self-talk." It is very important to state your affirmations (or suggestions) in the present tense and—as if they are—already a fact. For example; "I am so grateful and happy now that I have my own business."

Reframing is "re-stating" a previously *negative self-talk* statement or situation and then re-stating or seeing it from a different perspective. Reframes are more powerful when they are written down and are—at least a little more believable to us. For example; "I now see that having been fired from "ABC Company" allowed me the opportunity to start my own business— now I can chart my own life's course."

Literal and Inferred Affirmations

Some people respond better to *literal* affirmations or suggestions and other people respond more to an *inferred* affirmation. Once again, go with your feelings or emotional guidance on this. Does it *feel* good —is it neutral or—not *feel* good?

Here's the trick with affirmations. Our Subconscious mind does not hear negatives like our Conscious mind does. For example— if you say, "I am NOT fat"— it hears— "I am fat".

So, if it's a *weight issue* affirmation —then the *literal* statement could be something like—"I am my perfect weight of 150 pounds".

Here's the *inferred* version. "I *feel* healthier at my perfect weight of 150 pounds".

You will definitely respond better to one than the other. Even if you think you respond better to *literal* affirmations than *inferred* suggestions or affirmations— one will still *feel* more positive to you. Always check any tool you would like to use with your emotional guidance. Does it feel good? —or— Does it feel bad— or maybe— I can't tell! (it feels neutral).

Testing the Power of an Affirmation

A good way to test the power of an affirmation or a re-framed statement is to say it— over and over while exercising. For example, while *"power-walking"*— you could say something like this—"Money comes to me easily and effortlessly." If you begin to feel *stronger* as you repeat the affirmation— then you have dialed it in!

In fact, stating your affirmations while doing intense aerobic exercise is one of the *most powerful* self-hypnosis tools there is— especially if you exercise three to five days a week.

A good friend of mine, Dr. Donna Hamilton, founder of New Vistas International, a training center for Clinical Hypnotherapy and Neuro Linguistic Psychology in Reno, Nevada—highly recommends—exercise while stating affirmations.

> *"Physical exercise fuels affirmations with enthusiasm by supporting the discharge of emotional blockages, and harnessing the power of the present moment. - Donna Hamilton, MFT, PhD*

I agree with Donna and I often recommend saying affirmations while doing a little—*free-form dancing*—to energetic (not frantic) music for five to fifteen minutes while focusing on your *positive central ideas* or stating *positive* affirmations. The body movement combined with energetic music helps keep our *monkey mind* preoccupied and quiet— at least long enough to allow the positive suggestion to drop right through our mind gate and into our Subconscious mind. Again, check your affirmation or re-frame with your emotional guidance. Does it *feel* good or does it *feel* bad?

Self-Talk

I am a professional listener— which means, I get paid to listen. After listening to a patient or client for ten to fifteen minutes…. I can tell if their *negative self-talk* is habitual or transitory. Almost everybody, at one time or another has used negative self-talk but— unless they are *stuck* on the emotional tone scale between Blame and Revenge— it is usually transitory. Well actually…. that's not necessarily true. We can get *stuck* on the emotional tone scale anywhere below Boredom with habitual negative self-talk.

Most people are giving themselves *negative* affirmations or suggestions all day long. All that *self-talk* really is— are suggestions or affirmations of how we see ourselves and the world. And these suggestions come from our subconscious programs!

We must be very observant and aware of how we talk to ourselves, especially our negative self-talk. That is why I like using the phrase, "Look what I created!" rather than the often used critical phrases like "that was stupid"— "I can't do it"—"I can't afford that"—"I'll never be able to accomplish that"— "That is too hard"—"I am too old" or "He/She won't let me"…. So please, stop giving yourself these negative suggestions.

How to RESTORE an Emotional Tone

A quick way to *restore* a state of mind from a time in recent memory when you were *feeling* better is to visualize that positive moment in time and then *anchor* it into your Subconscious mind. This is accomplished by putting your left thumb and index finger together— then breathe-in deeply at least five times while stating to yourself the *feeling* or emotional tone of that memory. For example; Freedom— or—Boring—or —Passion—or—Love….while visualizing the memory! This is, without a doubt, one of the most powerful techniques there is to *shock* you into *present time* by using past memories. This technique dates back to Merlin! When used with the *Mind Gate process* it can be incredibly powerful and deserves careful consideration.

A word of caution to initiates: *Choose wisely the memory you will use!*

The Escape Button

When you have a negative train of thought or emotions running away with you (keeping you in deep hypnosis and a lower tone) you must be able to hit "the Escape Button". We must always have a way out if we can become *conscious* enough to be aware when we may be headed for or already are— going into what I sometimes call *unauthorized hypnosis*. In other words, if we feel we may be rowing our boat into a storm (negative emotional tone) we must have a way that we can quickly turn in another direction. This is an amazing and powerful affirmation for staying in present-time and staying out of hypnosis during our waking hours.

From now on, whenever you feel like you are sliding down the emotional tone scale try saying something like; "Stop, Stop!" —or— "Cancel, Cancel!"—or—"WAAAAIT AMIINIT!" Anything that will interrupt that train of thought or negative feelings is good!

You may ask, "How can I tell if this is happening when my state of mind is deteriorating for no obvious reason?"

That is the question of the millennia, is it not? Remember your *emotional guidance system?* My answer to this and probably any other questions that may arise in your Conscious mind will be pretty much the same— how are you *feeling* as you are asking these questions?

If you are having a challenge getting in touch with your feelings then it may be more practical, as soon as possible, to try and *re-frame* your internal conversation. Try writing down or say something to yourself that is more empowering but believable. For example, if you have ever caught yourself saying something to yourself like— "I'll never be able to do that." Try *re-framing* it by saying— "With the right training I could do that." Or if you have a habit of saying "I'm getting too old". Re-frame it and say, "With age comes wisdom"—or if you are thinking something like, "I can't afford that."—a great *re-frame* is, "There must be a way that I can afford that."

Re-framing is something that requires awareness of our negative self-talk. Most of us are not even aware of what we are saying that is negative because our programs do this automatically. When we criticize ourselves or others it is usually because a program is running but we have not learned to recognize it. So, pay attention and start noting your self-talk as well as your critical judgment of others.

Reducing Fear and Guilt

This is the biggie of all biggies. I had felt that I had covered this emotional tone in the greatest detail that I possibly could have in Chapter One: A Common Condition but, I have to say now, that everyone feels this emotion on so many different levels and in so many different ways that I had to address it more completely. Fear is our natural reaction to an immediate threat or imminent danger. We are born with two fears—the fear of falling and the fear of loud noises. As we develop and are able to run or fight we also develop fears of threatened annihilation or eminent threat to ours or others survival. Remember our cave-men ancestors when a saber toothed tiger showed up for dinner? Fear is a primitive emotion that can save our lives but when it gets stimulated and there is nowhere to run or nothing to fight, it will send us immediately into a waking hypnotic state or trance.

Fear is usually felt in the heart or solar plexus and sometimes in both places. Many of my clients have described it as stomach pain while touching their solar plexus. It appears to be most intense there... in the diaphragm. If you've ever had the wind knocked out of you then you know where this area of the body is!

If there is a lot of fear and it seems to be running away with you, then first— identify the emotion and state it in present-tense to yourself— something as simple as, "I'm afraid" can be enough— or— just imagine for a moment that your emotions are like a small child (because they are). What could you say to reassure the child and let it know that you hear what it is saying and feeling?

If you were a loving parent you wouldn't invalidate the child's reality by saying "You aren't afraid or there's nothing to be afraid of."

Remember the Subconscious mind does not acknowledge or hear the negatives in an affirmation— so the statement "You are (not) afraid" is heard as "You are afraid". This can serve to affirm the fear and can make it escalate.

A very powerful affirmation that validates the emotion but slows down the energy of any negative program that may be running is a statement of fact like— "You've been afraid before". This is an extremely powerful *inferred* affirmation and re-frame at the same time. The inference is— you've survived this emotion before, and you will survive it again. The affirmation "You've been afraid before" calms down the intensity of the emotion and allows or creates a small gap in our running stream of thoughts as they are dropping into the Subconscious. It is the *adult- you* or *parent-you* soothing the fearful *child-you*. The child wants desperately to have someone take control because Fear can grip us tightly and make us feel out of control.

Fear can make a lot of noise in our head and create a lot of physical discomfort and pain as well (read The Diagnosis in Chapter Two). If you tend to process information more literally, something like— "I am brave and optimistic" may feel better to you. All of this work with affirmations and re-frames is about parenting or re-parenting ourselves. As always, as long as these are stated in present-tense— are believable to you— and meet the litmus test of, making you *feel* better, then you have just re-parented yourself successfully.

Guilt is a *gut-wrenching* experience as well. In fact, it is probably as powerful as Fear in many instances. If you have a lot of guilt and haven't done anything to hurt anybody intentionally then you need to be very clear that it is always coming from a strong negative program, meaning, it was given to you when you were very young and suggestible. But, you must remember…it is *only* a program! It is usually felt in the stomach but can also be felt in the back and pelvis.

Oftentimes, shame is mistaken for Guilt. John Bradshaw, author of –"On the Family" makes the distinction between the *two* like this: (I'm paraphrasing him here) Guilt says, *I made a mistake* and what can I do to correct it or make up for it? Shame says— *I am a mistake*! The difference is huge! One is a normal response to a human mistake and the other has been *programmed* into us at an early age.

If you are feeling a lot of Guilt or shame— and it is running away with you—telling yourself something like— "You've felt this way before" is a statement of fact and serves as a *reality check*— creating a brief moment of silence or —space— away from the monkey mind and puts the emotion of Guilt a little more in perspective.

You may have to say "You've felt this way before"— to yourself —a few times until— the intensity of this emotion dies down a bit. This will help you to *observe* the emotion for what it really is and it will weaken its grip on you. John Bradshaw speaks of *shame* as *toxic guilt*. Re-parenting your-self with the use of affirmations like above helps to move us back into present-time. Guilt or *shame* is almost always about the past so that alone tells you it is a negative Subconscious program. Just knowing that will help you to *observe* it with more clarity and perspective.

If you want to use affirmations and re-frames with *the Mind Gate process,* they should be written down and kept as simple as you can make them.

Keep It Simple

I wouldn't suggest you do more than one or two affirmations or re-frames at a time because, if you are saying them to yourself during your visualization, it is harder to memorize more than one or two— and still be able to visualize.

Remember that our Subconscious programs can be easily stimulated with vocal affirmations when you are visualizing and especially when it's *your voice* doing the vocalization, even if it's your *silent vocalization* to your-self.

All hypnotherapists know that we are the most *suggestible* to our *own* voice. Some people however, are able to do this more easily and with practice you will also be able to say affirmations while meditating. Saying them to your-self while doing *the Mind Gate process* can be extremely empowering. Do not get discouraged if you are not able to do this right away. Again, as I always say, check it out with your emotional guidance. Does it feel good or does it feel bad?

My experience with affirmations is that they work best if used to *evoke an emotion* rather than a specific desire so, once again, going general is always your best bet. For example—

Inferred: "I always feel so much appreciation for nature. I feel calm when I visualize peaceful scenes".

Literal: "I am peaceful and appreciative. I am grateful to be alive".

Sometimes the difference can be very subtle but one will always feel a little better or ring a little truer to you. I have given some more examples of affirmations below. Some are literal and some are inferred.

NOTE: Be sure to always state your affirmations or suggestions as positive— and— in present tense. Say them as if the desired condition is a fact.

Examples:

Inferred: "I love the way exercise makes me look and feel".
"I feel motivated when I exercise".
Literal: "I exercise three times a week".
"I am stronger and looking great".

More Examples:

- I love the way exercise makes me feel. I feel motivated and I feel great.
- I enjoy eating healthy low calorie meals that keep my weight at xxx pounds.
- I get so excited when I see, smell, touch and feel my partner. I love making love to her/him and completely satisfying her/him.
- I am feeling so sexy whenever I see myself in the mirror.
- I love myself and I love my life.
- All the clutter is cleared away and I am organized.
- I am so happy and grateful now that_____.
- I am so happy now that I am organized and motivated to succeed/ meditate/ walk/plan my life, etc....
- I am grateful that my body knows how to heal itself.
- I am so relieved that my relationship with my wife/ husband/ girlfriend/ boyfriend/ daughter/ son is finally healed.
- I am healed, whole and healthy.
- Every day and in every way, I am getting better and better.

Reframes:

- I believe/ I have faith that I can be happy/ excited/ grateful/ relieved that_____.
- I am willing to be healed/motivated/excited to_____.
- I deserve_____.
- I am open to let _____ come into my life
- I can see now that what happened was for my higher good/ the higher good of all so I can let it go.

CHAPTER 5

Imagination

"Imagination is everything. It is the preview of life's coming attractions."

-Albert Einstein

The Power of Suggestion

So, the question now becomes; "How do we reprogram our Subconscious mind so that only our *positive* programs get stimulated?" I will discuss several ways to stop *negative* program— momentum— that has already been created and then how to start a momentum in a positive direction— and this is not just about *thinking positively*. Positive thinking, while being a great idea does not work very well on its own. There is way too much negative input coming into our Conscious mind from the *news* (Never Ending Worry Source) headlines and other sources (including our own negative thoughts) on a daily basis to try and negate such massive amounts of negative message units. By the end of the day we are often exhausted, overloaded and completely deep in hypnosis.

There's only one way to stimulate our Subconscious mind to *create* new positive programs— and that one way is through the *power of suggestion!* You must learn how to control that power or it will run amuck and cause all sorts of damage. Not controlling what *suggestions* get through the Mind Gate and into the Subconscious mind is like someone said once of politicians. It was either Will Rogers or Mark Twain that said, "Electing a politician to office is like giving a hammer to a four year old—you just hope you can get it away from him before he does too much damage".(Come to think of it, that could have been James Whitmore playing Will Rogers).

Anyway, you and only you hold *the key* to your Mind Gate, but if you allow "the gatekeeper" to fall asleep (go into trance) without your supervision, a variety of damage can occur. In other words, you must be aware of your Emotional Tone...all of the time!

To install *positive* suggestions into our Subconscious mind, We must be in a suggestible state of mind, in other words, be open-minded and willing (the Mind Gate must be open) to use our *imagination* to create positive images that the Subconscious mind will respond to. But, you must be awake as you use this process — in other words, you must be *conscious* while this is happening. Guard against overwhelm or overload. If you are feeling overwhelmed you are probably in or about to go into the state of hypnosis so you will need a quick way to snap out of it.

I've included a chapter (Chapter 7: How to De-Hypnotize Ourselves) about how to stay out of hypnosis in the book so please— read that— otherwise, it will be that much harder to get the results you want. In order for your Subconscious mind to respond to these *positive images*, they must carry a certain amount of positive emotional energy with them. When you are visualizing, imagining, or pretending a particular circumstance or scene it must *feel* good to you, or at least, feel much better than you have been feeling and, you must be able to sustain that picture and feeling for a few minutes each day.

The Best Times to Do the Process

Because we naturally go into the state of hypnosis before sleep and upon awakening, these are the easiest times to do the Mind Gate process. However, it is possible to do the process anytime during the day as well. Whichever time works best for you is okay but remember, originally the Subconscious mind was programmed through associations and identifications so you can try different times and places but soon you will want to settle down to one or two times and places.

The adult Subconscious mind also responds to the law of association and the law of repetition. Decide what works best for you and, as always, check with your emotional guidance to what *feels* the best to you. An easy chair, your bed or even a meditation cushion all work fine as long as you do not fall asleep during your session. I personally prefer to do *the process* first thing in the morning with my timer set for twenty to thirty minutes depending on how much time I have before I need to get ready for my day.

NOTE: If you are doing *the process* in bed it is best that you sit upright or semi-reclined with your back and neck well-supported with pillows.

Our *mind gate* or Critical mind only opens under certain circumstances. Normally, when we go to sleep, we go through the brain wave state of Theta or REM (rapid eye movement) also known as "hypnoidal" sleep. It is the state of detached awareness where we are not quite asleep but we are not quite awake. Remember, if the mind gate has had time to analyze all of the information (message units) from the days information, it will attach or direct any of those bits of information that are like your programs—good or bad— positive or negative to your current programs. (see Fig. 4)

Mind
Normal State

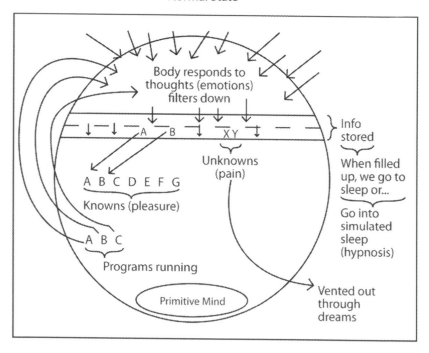

Fig. 4

When sleeping, mind gate opens & MU's drop through into subconscious (S.C.) if knowns. If unknown, they get vented out through dreams.

Before waking, you will have what are called venting dreams. These are often the ones you remember best because they occurred right before waking and are still fresh in your memory. While these dreams can be disturbing or not make any sense to you, keep in mind they are mostly made up from information that is not like any of our programs. They are thrown out like junk-mail or spam and so are considered superfluous information by the Subconscious mind. This is why they are vented out in the form of dreams. In fact, many neuropsychologists believe the purpose of sleeping —is to dream. Dreaming is much like de-fragging our computer to free up disc space. It releases energy back to us.

Some people have told me they don't dream but, unless you are kept from going into the Theta brain wave level (REM-rapid eye movement) by someone or something that keeps you from going into that state, you will dream, whether you know it or not. If you give your-self a suggestion to *remember* your dreams before sleep then you will remember your dreams or at least you'll have a vague memory that you did dream.

"Energy cannot be created or destroyed, it can only be changed from one form to another"-Albert Einstein

Everything is energy, including message units (MU's) that get vented out as dreams. The other time the mind gate opens naturally is when we are first waking up and our consciousness moves from the Delta brain wave (unconscious sleep) state and up through the levels toward awakening by way of Theta brain waves (REM) rapid eye movement again. We stay in that state about ten to twenty minutes before we come up into the Alpha (detached awareness) brain wave state a few minutes and then become fully conscious into the Beta brain wave or so-called waking state. So, the first thing after awakening is a good time to reprogram the Subconscious by visualizing with *positive* emotions what you want to feel or experience in life. In fact, this is probably the best time to do *the Mind Gate process* but you'll have to set a timer if you need to be somewhere— like work. Fantasizing is highly encouraged as long as it *feels* good to you so let the imagination run wild—along positive trails!

Alarming Awakenings

If you still use a loud annoying alarm clock that sounds like Neo's alarm from the movie, "The Matrix", please consider investing in something like an iPod or CD alarm so that you can choose the music you want to wake up to. I would highly recommend some gentle wake-up music. There is a reason they call alarm clocks "alarm" clocks. Set your new "gentle soft music wake-up device" for twenty to thirty minutes earlier so that you can go to the bathroom then quickly go to your meditation place and begin *the process.*

Set a kitchen timer for fifteen to twenty minutes before you begin. A kitchen timer works best because it's unlikely you'll sleep through its annoying sound. If you have nowhere to go then a kitchen timer is unnecessary. The first thing in the morning is ideal doing the process and starting your whole day out on the right foot. I highly recommend it. The only thing here is to make sure your wake up device is set loud enough to pull you out of the process because you will be in self-hypnosis. I've often stayed in meditation two hours when not using a timer.

On the other hand, if you aren't completely exhausted by the time you hit the sack, doing *the process* before going to sleep works well also.

Dr. John Kappas referred to the last half hour before we fell asleep as *the magic thirty minutes* because the Critical area or mind gate will *always* open before we go into unconscious sleep (delta brain waves). I would agree with him that when it comes to getting information that you want to have go into the Subconscious mind or giving your-self positive suggestions before sleep is good—but—first thing in the morning works best for *the Mind Gate process* because you have less to process in the morning or upon awakening. The Subconscious mind has already vented out a lot of superfluous message units (junk mail) and your Conscious mind has not been filled up with negative information yet.

That said, I do have to say that when you first start using *the Mind Gate process* it may be a good idea to do it at both times— as a safeguard against— dropping negative suggestions into the Subconscious when you are very tired and probably *overloaded* from the days input of message units. So, at least until you realize you are hanging-out or operating more in the upper tones on the emotional tone scale on a more consistent basis, it may be a good idea to do *the process* before sleep and upon arising.

I personally have had my best sessions first thing in the morning but I usually go to sleep meditating to beautiful music and balmy shores. With practice you'll quickly train yourself to go down into the alpha brainwave state of consciousness and then into the deeper level of theta brain wave state of consciousness without falling asleep. It's like the guy who was seeking directions, asked a fellow with a violin case on a New

York City street "Can you tell me how to get to Carnegie Hall?"—"Practice, practice, practice" the musician said.

There is a trick to doing this (going into theta for extended periods without falling asleep). I will show you this trick and with just a little practice, practice, practice you'll soon be a master at controlling your state of mind.

It is best, when you begin using *the Mind Gate process* that you keep your positive suggestions very general and not too specific. So, just imagine, picture or pretend that you are in a beautiful place or situation. Maybe it is a fantasy you've had or always wanted to have or maybe it's something or someplace that you remember where there were *good feelings*.

Hitch Hiking Ghosts

When using memories for visualizations, it is critical that you do not let any attached *negative* associations come into the visualization. I call these negative associations "Hitch Hiking Ghosts" (from Disneyland's Haunted Mansion ride). For example, if you see yourself playing with an old pet and a mental picture, feeling or thought pops up about the pets death it could then evoke an emotion of Grief.

That is why, in my opinion, fantasies work best, but if you decide to use a memory, just try to keep it on an endless *loop* of the happy feeling or edit it to be just the positive part of the memory.

NOTE: Don't allow any negative pictures, thoughts or feelings to come into your visualization time. If a negative picture, thought or feeling does wander in you can quickly *switch* to an *emergency backup picture* that feels good. It's a good idea to write these good-feeling pictures down on paper to make them more real to you.

Emergency Backup Picture

So, write down and/or practice switching to a pleasant scene as a back-up plan. Memories, as much as we love them, are often attached to a variety of *negative* emotions that we are not always consciously aware of. This is why many hypnotherapists, including myself, will *not* do "Regression" therapy. Regression therapy is where the client, under hypnosis is directed back to a time in their life where they may have "blank" spots or very obscure or dark memories. The subject is then given *suggestions* to "be there now."

The object is to find answers in the past to help resolve a current issue. It is potentially volatile and may open up a virtual Pandora's Box of negative memories and emotions. Personally I believe Regression therapy should only be done under strict supervision by a qualified psychotherapist who knows their client very well. So, use your common sense and consciously think about the happy memory for quite a while before you decide to use it with *the Mind Gate process*. In my practice and workshops I do not encourage using memories unless I need to help a client remember how to visualize, and then, for only moments and under my very careful guidance.

Fantasizing

A fantasy might look like this; imagine, picture or pretend you are lying on a massage table on a lanai in Hawaii. You are enjoying getting a massage (one of my personal favorites) and as you are imagining getting a massage, *see* if you can *feel* the feeling of your muscles relaxing under the massage therapist's hands. Allow your muscles to release tension as you *feel* or *imagine* the hands of the therapist moving over every part of your body. Imagine the massage therapist is starting with your feet then moving up to your calves and up to the back of your legs.... then up to your lower back muscles....now your middle back.... your neck and shoulder muscles....the massage therapist is now moving down your arms, pulling all the tension out of those muscles as they then move down....to the hands and fingers....feeling all the tension in your body drain.... right out through your fingers....as the therapist now moves up the back of your neck and scalp muscles you are feeling even more relaxation and appreciation....feeling the therapist's fingers now gently massaging your scalp and ears....releasing all the tension as you melt into the Joy of being alive....

Imagine, picture or pretend you are feeling a slight cool breeze wafting over your hair and perhaps the smell of tropical flowers like plumeria and the musky aroma of teak wood mixed with the subtle scent of ocean in the air.... Maybe you can hear the ocean or seabirds in the distance— Imagine now taking a sip of a tropical drink as the cool glass and ice touch your lips with the heady aroma of rum, pineapple and coconut wafting into your nose ....then as the liquid teases your tongue you begin feeling even more relaxed and warm .... Swishing the juice around in your mouth a moment to take in all the flavors as the elixir floods your taste buds with paradise ....then swallowing and noticing that warm feeling flow through every part of your body as the muscles relax and let go.... even more....there are the sounds of Hawaiian music faintly drifting in and out in the background.

You'll want to incorporate as many of the five senses as you can into your fantasy to make it as real as you can. Your Subconscious does not know the difference between reality and fantasy so it will just respond by running programs that are like your fantasy. Again, the more real you can make this picture and the more *good-feeling* emotions you can elicit from your visualization— the stronger the suggestion will be to your Subconscious mind to run programs that are *like* your visualization.

As this happens over a period of time and on a regular basis these fantasies or *symbols* of relaxation and happiness will become thoughts in our Conscious mind that elicit calm, relaxing and soothing feelings in the body. The body will respond to these thoughts with good-feeling emotions and your state of mind will rise to higher and higher levels on the scale automatically! As you begin to *hang-out* in the higher tones of the scale it will become easier and easier to reach the highest tones or what I like to call *mind orgasms*.

Images and Patterns

So, let's look at the Emotional Tone Scale Again. It is critical that you understand how your emotional tone or state of mind creates your experiences and your physical reality or your world. Many, if not all *spiritual* teachers will say that Joy is our natural state and— when we quit resisting that state, by ridding ourselves of negative thoughts then we will bounce right back up to our natural state of Joy automatically. Think of babies! Unless they need food or their diaper changed they are in a state of joy. Go to "google images" and type in "laughing babies". Or again, for some real belly laughs— go to YouTube and type in "Laughing Babies". It's a hoot!

Thoughts become habitual and are often accompanied by our own little mind movies and images. It's important to remember that our emotions trigger more of the same kind of thoughts! We have developed *patterns* of thought because, according to neuroscientists, *neurons that fire-together — wire-together* so, to interrupt these old patterns we must give the Subconscious mind regular input (law of repetition) and preferably at the same times of day or evening and preferably in the same place (law of association).

You now know that you go into hypnosis when you go to sleep and again when you come out of sleep so that gives you two times that work great for this process. The goal here is to be able to raise your emotional tone for at least ten to fifteen minutes a day. That will start a *neural-net* re-wire in the brain that will actually create a whole new pattern and even a whole new YOU in only a few weeks. But, the good news is that even within a few days, you will begin to notice positive changes in how you *feel* and begin to *see* evidence of changes in your outside world. Colors will be a little brighter— people will begin to respond to you in a more positive way because you will be attracting people who vibrate or resonate at your new emotional tone level. You may not even (or barely) notice those people who are on a lower tone level.

A Sure Sign It's Working

A sure sign that *the Mind Gate process* is working and that your Subconscious mind is making the changes you want is that— you will have more early-morning dreams or more dreams before waking which, if you remember, are called *venting* dreams. This means that your Critical mind or the mind gate is doing what it's supposed to be doing!

So, your goal is going to be imagining— visualizing— or pretending that you can see images that will evoke strong positive emotions from the top six levels on the emotional tone scale.

Emotional Tone Scale

1. Joy—Empowerment—Freedom—Love-Appreciation
2. Passion for another—Passion
3. Enthusiasm-Eagerness—Happiness
4. Positive expectation—Positive beliefs
5. Optimism
6. Hopefulness
7. Contentment
8. Boredom
9. Pessimism
10. Frustration-Irritation-Impatience
11. Disappointment
12. Doubt
13. Worry
14. Blame
15. Discouragement
16. Anger
17. Revenge
18. Hatred—Rage
19. Jealousy
20. Insecurity—Guilt—Unworthy
21. Fear—Grief—Despair.

Feel It in Your Body

Do not be disappointed if you cannot feel a higher emotion at first. In fact, at first you may not be able to *feel* any emotion at all. That is perfectly alright as long as you continue to work on a picture or visualization of a pleasant scene because the emotions will start to come as your Subconscious mind begins to float little positive *thought-bubbles* up to your Conscious mind. Remember your body responds to these so-called thoughts with emotion— so the process will happen quite naturally. Try to get in touch with what part of your body feels these emotions. Is it in the area of the heart, the solar plexus, the stomach, the groin or someplace else? How does your body feel when you think of something exciting? Learn to get the connection between the body and the mind by observing your thoughts and feelings. Where do we *feel* things anyway? *We feel with our body!*

The Nature of Reality

Our emotions act just like a powerful radio transmitter and will attract to you those circumstances, people, places and things that are in that very same emotional tone level!

For example, if you feel Angry a lot, you'll notice a lot of angry people in your world. Everywhere you look there will seem to be angry people or angry dogs or even angry birds.

It is absolutely critical that you understand how important it is for you to feel good emotionally!

I don't know any other way to say this other than you must realize by now that you are a "reality-creating" being! You create your reality through your emotions....

It (your reality) is all you! It is you who created your physical world! It is you that created your perceived reality through your programs, so if you don't like what you are experiencing, then learn how to simply change the channel!

If you are habitually looking outside your-self at the world and seeing things that Disappoint you, or make you Doubt who you are— or Worry or— have a judgment about people, governments or companies that are to Blame for your circumstances then— you will keep seeing those things in *your* world. And *your* habitual thoughts will cause interference patterns that will affect *my* world, to a greater or lesser degree depending on how close you are to me.

Yes I know, there are some people (maybe you) reading this material that may be saying to themselves—

"Yeah, well, if I think like that then I'll be living in a dream world. If I start being Optimistic or turn my back to all the bad things happening in the world then I'll be lying to myself." But quantum physics and neuroscience tells us— if we do not start living in that *dream-world*, or as some might say, "lying to ourselves", we will never draw into our experience anything above what we are feeling and thinking about right now!

Nothing will change for the better because reality is not "out there". Reality is "in here" where you live— emotionally. Think about this a moment. How are you feeling right now? Are you feeling good, feeling bad or just feeling neutral? Next, notice what you are thinking about. I guarantee that what you will begin to feel, very shortly will be a mirror image of those thoughts emotionally.

Dr. Victor Frankl, a Viennese psychiatrist wrote an amazing book called "Man's Search for Meaning". It's about how to survive a Nazi prison camp in world war two (WWII). It is all about the necessity of living in a *dream-world*. He would know because he beautifully documented his own personal experience in a Nazi prison camp! He survived when others who succumbed to the emotional tones of Despair perished. He did this by having happy thoughts about his life before the war. He would go over every detail of his life with his wife and family before he went to sleep and would *fantasize* about how they would laugh and hug when they were reunited. Unbeknownst to him his wife had died in another camp and both his parents were killed by the Nazis. His sister was the only one of his family, besides him, that survived by escaping from Austria and from there then emmigrated to Australia.

In the movie called "Life is Beautiful", a father had smuggled his young son with him when he was taken to a Nazi prison camp in World War II. The father knew that, if discovered by the Nazis, his son would be taken to another camp and most likely perish. To protect his son he created an elaborate game of *hide and seek* (actually the game was more like hide from the Nazis). Whenever the son would question his father why no one else seemed to know or acknowledge the game was going on, his father would convince him that this was a *special* game and that they were very fortunate to be able to play this game and that everyone else *was* in on it but part of the game was not to let anyone else know they knew.

The way you won the game was to *not be found* by any of the soldiers, or any other people that could rat them out. He made sure that his son lived in a d*ream world*, a world of Joy and Freedom, a world of Love and Appreciation and especially, Empowerment.

They were playing a game and the competition was tough (the Nazi soldiers) and so they must have a *game plan* (a central idea) to win the game. The father knew if he allowed his son to *not* live in a *dream world* they would both perish. His son would be caught and most assuredly they would both die. This charade began to become *reality* for the father as well as he continued to use his imagination to direct his son's attention away from the cruelty and harsh *reality* of the prison camp. As bad as the conditions were in the Nazi prison camps, they found beauty and goodness all around them. Other people in the camp would protect and hide the child from the Nazis, even if they didn't want to! They had *no choice* because their (the father and His son's) energy was too big (high on the emotional tone scale). This is the correct interpretation and application of turning the other cheek. It was like "The Force" in the Star Wars movies. The force was definitely with them.

> "The Force has a powerful influence on the weak-minded."—Obi wan Kenobi

You must remember how to imagine and how to dream *consciously* and how to pretend if you are ever to experience The states of Joy, Freedom, Love, Appreciation and Empowerment on a regular basis. Once you've reached the emotional tone level of Hopeful for a few weeks—your momentum will be unstoppable and then moving even higher up the scale will be very rapid.

NOTE: You must stop being so practical about what you want and begin fantasizing— like when you were a small child. You must learn to have fun again with your greatest tool for change—your imagination!

What Does Visualization Do?

A mental picture or visualization can only be done in the conscious state and under the right conditions so that when it drops down into the Subconscious mind it becomes symbols of emotions or feelings. These symbols then will stimulate or activate your positive programs or become new positive programs with enough repetition.

Visualizations that evoke the higher emotional tones or feelings will activate *like* programs that create higher tone *thought bubbles* that percolate up to the Conscious mind as thoughts which can carry images or movies themselves. As the feedback loop occurs the body reacts to those thoughts with emotions which then creates more feelings or emotions that create more message units that eventually will become our way of experiencing our world.

Positive Vibes

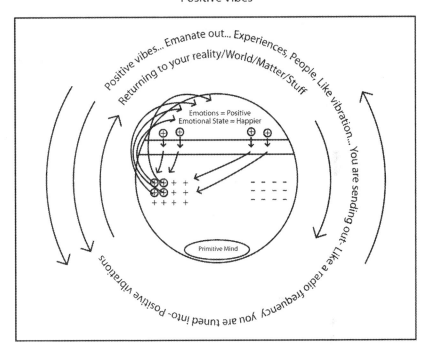

Fig. 7

Positive thoughts cause positive emotions.

Negative Vibes

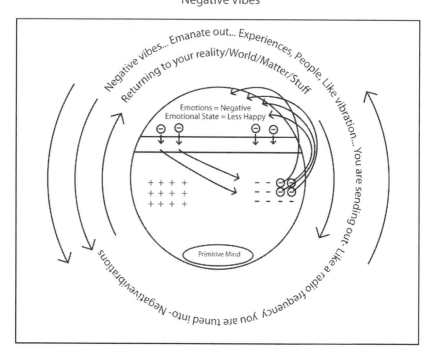

Fig. 8

Negative thoughts cause negative emotions.

In other words, our reality is being created over and over again unless we break the cycle or interrupt the circuits of these neural pathways or feedback loops (see Figs. 7 & 8). So, which *programs* do you want to *activate?* Remember, your Subconscious mind does not reason or decide which programs should be activated— only our Conscious mind gets to decide that by the thoughts and feelings it entertains or puts its attention on.

It's vital—no actually—it's crucial to your well-being and to the well-being of the world that you find a way to experience the higher levels of the emotional tone scale to keep your state of mind as positive as it possibly can be if you are to create "a beautiful life" for yourself and for those that you love. And indeed, your efforts will ripple out across the universe like a rock dropped in a clear pond. Your beautiful offerings will reach the distant shores of the universe and affect everyone and everything in a very positive way.

Quantum Computer Model

Basically, our Subconscious mind is like a supercomputer or "quantum" computer and our Conscious mind is like the monitor so we can see what we are creating. If you want to have good thoughts and good feelings you must be feeding your Subconscious mind good thoughts and feelings! There is no other way to do this.

There's an old computer axiom; GIGO, that is garbage in—garbage out.

By now it must be clear to you that our mind is very much like a computer, a *bio-computer* if you will, that can actually be re-programmed to create the life we want but, we must do this consistently, and we must really *care* about how we feel emotionally. I can't stress this enough.

You may have to change some bad habits you've developed over the years. You may have to stop hanging-out in certain places, stop reading certain material or listening to certain broadcasts, or maybe even, stop hanging- out with certain people. You must stop entertaining any thoughts, whatsoever— that are anything less than— what you truly want to show up in your life!

If you want to know what you have been thinking about on a consistent basis, or what your *thought-patterns* have been habitually, then go ahead and really look at your world and your reality of the world at large. Are you absolutely thrilled with what you see? If so, then throw this book in the trash because, you are there! Or, perhaps it may be more accurate to say you like some of what you experience and don't like other things you experience. However, if you are not thrilled at what you see and what keeps showing up consistently in your world, then read on because there is room for improvement.

What I am saying is that we need to take a long hard honest look at the patterns in our lives, including our *thought-life*. Are you constantly amazed or entertained and excited by what comes to you and what shows up in your life? Or, do you dread the morning and what the day may bring? Perhaps you are Hopeful in the morning and by lunchtime filled with Despair or Anger or Irritation.

Do you catch yourself Blaming the economy for your woes? Do you often find yourself in conversations about how Disappointed you are in our current administration and the state of our country or even the world? Or— maybe things are great in your world and you just want them to be even greater!

Researchers in neuroscience (brain science) are now observing that positive physical changes can occur with as little as ten to fifteen minutes of keeping our mind on a *central positive idea* for a few weeks. The brain can and will literally change its *shape* (neuroplasticity). This means that your *perceived reality* and *physical world*, including your physiology, can be transformed and manifested, as reality, in your physical world. Brain researchers and neuroscientists are discovering that the brain can actually change its shape in as little as eight weeks and has been documented using brain imaging like magnetic resonance imagery (MRI)!

Depending on the strength of your *positive feelings* and your ability to keep yourself focused on what you want and how it would feel to have it—changes can occur and usually do—much sooner than eight weeks. I've had many clients who once they get the hang of the process see major positive changes within a few days. For a detailed description of how this works, read Dr. Joe Dispenza's book, "Breaking the Habit of Being Yourself".

> "Everything is energy and that's all there is to it. Match the frequency of the reality you want and you cannot help but get that reality. It can be no other way. This is not philosophy. This is physics."- Albert Einstein

A Central Idea

Most of us cannot possibly imagine focusing on a central idea for ten to fifteen minutes without our minds wandering but, it can be done. On the other hand, according to Esther Hicks as the "channeled beings" called "Abraham", it only takes sixty eight seconds of *focused thoughts* and *feelings* to achieve this goal. Yes, I know I said ten to fifteen minutes because it usually takes that long to calm down our *monkey mind* before we can visualize and begin to feel how we want to *feel*.

Initially, start by visualizing something wonderful for seventeen seconds. After doing that for a few days in a row you will be able to hold on to your *positive visualization* for an even longer period of time. The important thing here is to be able to experience this positive visualization enough to elicit or stimulate an emotional tone or *feeling* at one of the higher levels. In other words, you'll Want to be shooting for—at the very least—the *feeling* of Hopefulness.

Visualization just helps you to stimulate these higher emotional tones. Once you can feel Hopefulness on a fairly regular basis, it is an easy step up to the tone of Optimism and even easier to reach the tones of Positive expectation and beliefs. When you have that tone nailed you'll almost fall up to Enthusiasm, Eagerness and yes, even Happiness. Once you have felt and experienced these feelings, there is absolutely no stopping you from rising or floating up to Passion...and when you are at Passion for a time, it won't be long before you will catapult yourself into Appreciation. When you can appreciate all the good in your life you will be looking for things to appreciate all the time because that emotional tone creates Joy for you. After some consistent practice with *the Mind Gate process*, you will be able to hold your visualizations and feelings easily for sixty eight seconds!

Sixty-Eight Seconds

Only Sixty eight seconds of sustained and focused thought and feelings is the goal! Why only sixty eight seconds? Because, that is the time it takes for your brain's neurons to fire 21 times! The actual number is 3.14159265359 X 21. In other words, pi. It is commonly known as the ratio of a circle's circumference. In other words, it is a complete cycle. That the universe is completely mathematical is no news to scientists. In fact, it was around 250 B.C.E. that Archimedes observed the mathematical precision of the movement of the stars around the earth.

So, what about Contentment, you may say? It is an easy slide down from Contentment to Boredom and then our *monkey mind* starts looking for something to entertain itself and it's not usually looking for something in the higher registers on the emotional tone scale. It loves dragging up our past mistakes or worries about the future —so if you find yourself going there you will know it is trying to figure out some program that bubbles up a negative thought.

Sometimes our *monkey mind* may seem or even *feel* a little positive— but it won't be long before it's got you sucked into a thought-stream that will invariably lead to negative feelings. So, watch that little sucker because it's clever— but you are a lot smarter than you know.

Remember that Hopefulness is the feeling you'll want to focus on initially. The higher registers on the emotional tone scale are sometimes a little difficult to reach at first— but it won't take very long however before you are moving up the scale. So don't become discouraged because you are learning a new skill here and all it takes is a little patience and persistence and you'll get there much sooner than you might imagine.

As you reach Hopefulness and keep doing *the process* in a few days to a few weeks— your reality will begin changing from where it was— to where it can be more quickly than you may have ever thought possible.

Monkey Mind

Your Conscious mind contains all the *chatter* or so-called *thoughts* that are going on in your awareness and is what I call— the "monkey mind". It is constantly chattering about what it has its attention on at any given moment. This can be environmental awareness, like the room temperature, our own body sensations as well as information in the form of *thoughts* that *bubble* up from the Subconscious mind (programs).

It bounces around all over the place and is always *thinking, thinking, thinking* and trying to *figure out* our problems and dilemmas. It can take many years of meditative practice to get the Conscious *monkey mind* to calm down enough to introduce a new idea — and then have it delivered *strongly and intact* into the Subconscious mind without using *the Mind Gate process.*

Hypnotherapy

In hypnotherapy, the Conscious mind becomes *overloaded* by the words of the hypnotherapist. As a result, all of these words, expressed as ideas and pictures cause the Critical mind or mind gate to become overloaded and then disorganize or open up. When the mind gate disorganizes all of the accumulated MU's (message units) drop into the Subconscious mind— without analyzing the information— and the hypnotherapist' *positive* suggestions go in too!

However, the most recent *suggestion* will be the strongest and will be the one acted upon by the very powerful Subconscious mind. If that idea or suggestion is accepted by the Subconscious mind then the Subconscious mind will act on that suggestion and those positive ideas or information will then *bubble* up into our Conscious mind as *thoughts.*

Those thoughts cause our body to respond with emotions (energy in motion) and that is how change is accomplished with hypnotherapy. *The Mind Gate process* incorporates *self-hypnosis* along with *yoga, diaphragmatic* breathing, *meditation* and *visualization* techniques. With *the Mind Gate process*, you can accomplish amazing changes by simply allowing yourself the time— before sleep— or first thing after awakening— while the *mind gate* is still disorganized— to introduce a *central idea (suggestion)* and block some of the *monkey mind's* chatter.... with music.

For example— a positive suggestion can be a picture or image of getting a massage in Hawaii—like I described before—or any pleasant fantasy is good as long as it gives you the feeling you want. You may not like getting massages so it is okay to have anything else that feels good in your visualization. Anything that makes you feel any positive emotion whatsoever like: Optimism—Hopeful— Enthusiasm— Happiness—Eagerness or even Passion for another person or cause— is all good.

When you are able to visualize something that makes you feel the highest levels of human experience such as Joy— Freedom—Appreciation or Love on a regular basis— then you will have Empowered yourself to receive whatever good things await you at those *frequencies*. And the law of attraction will bring to you, as Jesus said; "....even greater things than these".

This is what real Empowerment is because —it is You who is *empowering* yourself! You will be literally *taking* your power back and then know that you are, and always have been—the creator of your reality! You will be *re-programming* your Subconscious mind to create all the bounty and the beauty in your physical world that you have always wanted.

Why Raise Our Emotional Tone?

So why would you want to raise your emotional tone besides— just to feel better? Do you remember my story in Chapter Two- The Diagnosis? Because of my higher emotional tone (state of mind) following my surgery and recovery I *attracted* information through a colleague of mine that increased my abundance— easily by tenfold!

My chiropractic practice took off like a rocket and so did my income. But, because *I am* a creator, I kept right on creating. I created mostly *good stuff*— but it always seemed to be mixed with some *bad stuff* as well because— I was missing the information I needed— the *Mind Gate* information— that I am now giving you in this book. Had I known then what I know now, life would have been very, very, very different for me—and others.

The Secret to Getting What You Really Want

So, what is it—that you really want? What are your goals— your hopes and your dreams?

If you have something you really want and you know what that is, that's great, but— if your wants are more general, such as— better health— better relationships— better income or maybe even just —more free time— then that is great also! In fact, doing *the Mind Gate process* to just raise your *emotional tone* is really all you may ever need to do— because of the most wonderful *secret* of all!

The secret is this: ever since you arrived on this planet you have been exposed to *contrast*— or— as the Buddha might say; "*the field of duality*". The earth-plane is all about contrast and duality such as; good or bad— right and wrong— hot or cold— moral and immoral— North and South— Democrat vs. Republican— tastes good or tastes bad—smells good or smells bad, etc… It goes on and on and on. That is how we created our subconscious programs in the first place!

When I discussed Theory of Mind with you, you may remember your Subconscious mind learned by *associations* and *identifications*— through—the laws of association, identification and repetition. For example— you might associate chocolate cake with feeling loved or happy or you may associate chocolate cake with feeling sick to your stomach— depending on your exposure to chocolate cake (especially before the age of eight years old).

Or—you might *associate* eating chocolate cake with the negative feeling of Guilt because— your mother may have caught you sneaking some chocolate cake and— may have chastised you and told you what a "bad little person" you were. Chances are good that you don't even remember most of these associations and identifications— but, I can assure you, they are there ("…25,000 hours of pure conditioning in early childhood just from verbal cues alone"-Deepak Chopra).

So, here's **the real secret**—every experience you've ever had has been judged—by you—to be either good or bad. And, if they are *bad* experiences—the bigger part of you then wishes for something better. That *wish* becomes a *thought* that has an *emotion* attached to it—which goes *somewhere* into your energy field. And, it still exists as a potential reality or possibility! This is pure quantum physics because—it (the wish) is still existing somewhere as *energy* in your energy field or perhaps your higher-self, your body or even—in a parallel universe.

"Energy cannot be created or destroyed, it can only be changed from one form to another"- Albert Einstein

There are places in your energy field that are literally full of wishes (bundles of energy) you've had over the years and are *trapped* in a sort of *emotional energy escrow account.*" Abraham, channeled by Esther Hicks calls this our *vibrational escrow or— the vortex.*

For example— if someone is rude to you and you wish they were not rude, your mind will catalog that wish of wanting to experience *love* instead of rudeness. *Love* is a very high emotional tone or *vibration.* Or—let's say you really wanted a motor-scooter when you were younger. You may have *identified* or *associated* motor-scooters with the emotions of Freedom or, perhaps even—Joy. The desire you may have had of riding the motor-scooter and feeling those wonderful feelings also got *cataloged* away in your *emotional escrow account.*

Since you are connected to (one with) the *unified field* as an *energy field* yourself— your wishes and desires are *held* for you— much like backing up your computer to *the cloud.* Anything you have ever wanted, or at least its *essence* (the feeling of having it) is there, in your energy field and it is just waiting for your *state of mind* to rise to the emotional tone associated with it. It exists in the unified field as a *possibility,* according to quantum physicists. You need only learn how to *tune-in* to its emotional tone or frequency!

This is likened to tuning your radio to the correct station. If you want to listen to 98.7 and you tune to 88.7— you will not hear the station you want to hear. By the same token, if you want all the *good stuff* available at the emotional tone of Appreciation but you are only able to *feel* the emotional tone of Optimism, then you will not see evidence (manifestation) of the emotional tone of Appreciation in your reality. It just won't show up! Or, for example, if you want people to feel Appreciation for what you are or do— but are only able to *feel* Optimistic— you may attract a lot of *optimistic* people or situations into your life—few, if any— who appreciate you!

So, all you have to do is *hold* an emotional tone or state of mind consistently— for a short time. How long is a short time? Most teachers agree that you need to hold an *emotional tone level*— or a *thought* that evokes the *emotional tone* of what you want for approximately ten to fifteen minutes a day— for at least twenty-one days in a row. Again, there are some who say you need to hold the emotional tone or feeling for only sixty eight seconds per day— for twenty-one days.

I would agree that you only need to *feel* or hold the emotional tone or feeling of what you want for only sixty eight seconds— however, it will take a few minutes to settle down the *monkey mind* enough to experience the *feeling* of what you want. Twenty-one days is a kind of *magic number* that you will want to shoot for. It is really the law of repetition. Remember, the universe (and you are a part of the universe) is mathematical (there's pi again). However, that does not mean that you could not manifest something you want much sooner than that, especially if you can put a lot of emotional energy into it. But, that said, spiritual teachers as well as neuropsychologists and neuroscientists are usually referencing the manifestation of something specific.

So— here's the deal. If you will just have a little faith or trust in the energy that maintains the universe—or if you prefer, your *higher-self* or *God*, etc.to bring you anything, or the *essence* (the feeling of having whatever it is that you want) of anything positive that may be in your emotional escrow account, I would say— go for it! You'll start to see evidence of it working much more quickly because —you will not be obsessing over or be addicted to some *specific item* showing up in your physical world. A great way to prove this to your-self is to do the first experiment in Pam Grout's book, E-SQUARED. Just ask that God show you a sign!

The reason I say this is because, when you are focused on a specific item or situation coming to you, it is easier to *slide down* the emotional tone scale into Disappointment before the item(s) shows up in your physical world. The emotional tone of Disappointment can pull you down easily into Doubt and Worry—like holding a cork down under the water. If you are feeling *disappointed* about your desire not manifesting, I guarantee you, it will not— not in the way you want it to. What will show up are more *disappointing* parades of people and situations filing into your life!

This happens to a lot of us when we first start doing this kind of *transformational work*. Rather than trying to manifest a specific item, person or situation, it is far better to work on our state of mind. Doing that alone— will attract all the good stuff that is in our emotional escrow account already!

Whatever it takes for us to feel better emotionally is what we need to be focused on. So don't sweat the specifics of what you want, instead— go for the **feeling** of what you want. In other words, if you want a better job—ask yourself; "how would it *feel* to have that better job?" Why we want—what we want— is always about *the feeling* of the desire being realized, or manifested, in our physical world. In other words, we know we will feel better when we have this thing we want! For example—if we want a new car, we must ask ourselves first, "What will I *feel* when I get the new car?" Then, if we can experience that *feeling* or *hold* that feeling *consistently* and strongly for only sixty eight seconds— twenty one days in a row—the car will be on its way to you or has already manifested and is now sitting in your driveway!

The Deeper Secret

You'll be able to easily peg that *feeling* of owning the new car on the emotional tone scale. When you do the process with your visualization, you will know exactly what *feeling* to go for. If visualizing or *seeing* yourself driving the new car generates a strong enough *positive* emotional tone in you (Joy—Empowerment—Freedom—Love—Appreciation—Passion—Enthusiasm—Eagerness—Happiness) and, if you can sustain that tone for ten to fifteen minutes a day (or at least solidly for 68 seconds) for a few weeks—then great, go for it! However, if you are doing *the Mind Gate process* with the sole intention of just, raising your emotional tone, there will be amazing positive *side-effects* (actually direct effects) and you will be cultivating tones of Appreciation for all that you already have. *The Mind Gate process* may then become for you— a prayer of gratitude because you will attract whatever is in your *emotional escrow account* or something— even better will manifest that is like the *essence* or *feelings* of— what is in your emotional escrow account at those emotional tone levels!

Either way, it can be (and probably will) be even better than you could ever imagine. So, have fun with this, and go for the *feelings* of Joy and Empowerment because you will experience and feel the Freedom you've always craved.

We always want to *appreciate* all of the love that's coming to us from our source—in the form of friends, events, material wealth and circumstances, even if we can't see how that may happen.

Whenever we encounter a kind clerk at the grocery store, a helpful bank teller or some person who goes above beyond their duty to help us in some way and we felt Appreciation of the service we have received, we radiate out to the Universe that emotional tone—drawing more of the same feelings to us. When you've mastered the emotional tone scale, you'll be pretty much able to manifest anything you want and — very quickly.

The Balloon "Guided" Visualization

I wrote The Balloon story as a *guided imagery* to use specifically for those who have a *working knowledge* of the emotional tone scale. I was doing *the Mind Gate process* one morning not long ago when this story came to me in a vision. After being deep in trance for nearly two hours, I came out of hypnosis with a warm feeling throughout my body that cannot be described as anything other than pure Love and Appreciation. I was so moved that I asked my wife Terri to listen as I described, in as much detail as I could remember about the vision I experienced.

As I was recounting the images to her, tears began to flow from my eyes and those images stimulated even more intense feelings of Love and Appreciation. My body was literally *quaking* within as a deep laughter filled my core. I remembered that feeling—it was the feeling of Joy! Then, I began to notice a part of me— trying to suppress that feeling.

Then Terri said "Wait", as she put her *smart phone* on video record. "Go ahead", she urged. I continued with her encouragement but was *choking up* with joyful emotions that I could hardly speak. Finally, I regained enough composure to continue with the story of my vision.

The feelings I was experiencing were a combination of how I felt when my children were born and when Terri agreed to marry me so many years before. I also remembered feeling these feelings when I heard other musicians playing music I had composed in a recording studio many years before. The feelings were Happiness on the highest level. Then I remembered these feelings as the same ones I experienced when I saw Terri walking down the aisle when we were married and how I couldn't quit grinning. In other words, that feeling that I was trying to describe was as close to pure bliss as I have ever experienced. It was what I call a *psychic* or *mind-orgasm*! You may want to read through The Balloon story a couple of times and then read through the emotional tone scale again. This guided imagery can easily *lift* you up the scale.

So, read or record the following and then visualize the story.

The Balloon is also available in a narrated form on Mp3 as a free download on my website. DrMitchellMays.com

The Balloon

Imagine, picture or pretend that you are walking in a beautiful green field of clover. You feel the softness of the carpet of clover as it gives way under your steps and notice the moisture collecting on your shoes from the dampness—left by the dew. There is a light, slightly cool breeze that plays with your hair and gently brushes your face. The sun is burning low in the eastern sky as you inhale the sweet crisp— early morning air. There are a few clouds floating across the pale gray-blue sky. The sounds of birds in nearby trees provide a contrasting background to the early morning quiet when suddenly you hear a *whoosh* from powerful propane burners. It is a perfect day for ballooning— and as you look to the west just up ahead there is a small hill.

On top of that hill, not more than a hundred feet away is a magnificent hot air balloon, now almost fully inflated. Its nylon envelope appears metallic with beautiful gold and silver stripes that run the length of the balloon from the parachute vent to the skirt. This is clearly no ordinary hot-air balloon. As you approach more closely you notice there are several ropes tied to the gondola or basket of the balloon with heavy bags of sand at the other end of the ropes and laying on the ground. The bags of sand surround the gondola, except where the entry door is located. The basket floats above the ground maybe six to eight inches as the heavy bags of sand act as anchors to keep the balloon from lifting off the ground. There are no crew around, only the bags of sand and the balloon pilot.

The door to the gondola is open and the pilot signals you to come aboard. You step inside as the balloon pilot is checking the instruments and pressure gauge but she needs your help.

"How can I help you" you ask, shouting above the noise of the burners. She points to the open door and so you reach out and latch the door closed. She then points to the ropes that are tied to mooring cleats inside the basket. She fires the burners again as the basket begins to shudder now but is unable to lift from the ground. The pilot is once again pointing at the ropes, but more fervently this time.

You notice that attached to each rope is a ribbon. Each ribbon has different words printed on it. The rope she is pointing to has a ribbon with the words *Fear* and *Grief* printed in black letters on a white ribbon. She makes signs with her free hand to untie the rope and throw it overboard. You struggle to untie the rope, but it's difficult to untie because it is knotted so badly and it resists your efforts. As you struggle with the rope the pilot is watching you and finally speaks.

"Get that rope untied— she shouts—or we'll never get off the ground." You work frantically to untie the rope from its cleat and are beginning to feel Frustration and Irritation, but the knot still will not budge.

"Get that rope untied— now!" the pilot shouts, even more loudly and with an urgency that is impossible to ignore.

Anger is beginning to well up— inside of you. Once again you pull at the knotted rope, harder and harder, and even harder. You feel the *Anger* as the adrenaline is flooding through your body and your heart races as you become even more determined to loosen the rope. The *Anger* feels powerful and it gives you more strength when finally—the knot begins to release. Still feeling strength of that emotion, the knot loosens and then finally comes undone. You watch as the rope and the ribbon that says F*ear* and G*rief*— slip over the side of the basket. The balloon suddenly jerks and shifts and you feel the basket rise a few feet.

The sudden movement of the basket throws you off balance and you fall onto the floor of the gondola. Sitting back on the floor of the basket with your arms and hands stretched out behind you, the pilot shouts out at you again— "it's lifting!" and smiles at you broadly. The balloon has only moved a couple of more feet when the pilot points to the other ropes. You look at the rope with the ribbon that says *Insecurity—Guilt*—and *Unworthiness* written on it. She signals you again to untie the rope.

Getting yourself up and off the floor of the basket quickly, you find that this rope is also knotted-up tightly but gives way a more easily as you are still feeling the power of *Anger.* The knot releases and you watch it slip over the side. The basket shudders—rising up a few feet more before stopping once again. The pilot is shaking her arm and pointing to the other ropes.

With the power of the Anger still pumping adrenalin into your body you go to work on the other ropes. Quickly and easily untying *Jealousy—Hatred—Revenge— Discouragement— Blame—Worry—Doubt—Disappointment—Frustration— Irritation—*Impatience—*Pessimism—Boredom* and even *Contentment!* "Whew" you say wiping the sweat off your brow.

Looking around the gondola you notice there are no more ropes left to untie, but the balloon has only risen a few more feet. The pilot is pulling the handle that operates the valve allowing more propane to ignite. The balloon strains to lift as the hot air bulges at the seams of the nylon envelope to near-bursting. Hot air is escaping through the parachute valve at the top and the balloon is straining and struggling to lift— pulling upward but still barely moving.

The pilot then glances back at you with an amused but somewhat empathetic look and shouts again above the roar of the burners —"let go of the anger!"

"What?" you say.

"I said— let go of the anger!" pointing to the last rope in your hand. You look down at your hand and see the rope wound around and around your arm. At the end of the rope there is a black ribbon with big red letters that spell the word *Anger*. The feeling of *Anger* is so powerful and strong that you are already feeling some anxiety at the realization that you have to let it go. You unwind the rope from your arm, but your grip on the rope tightens and you still hold onto it with your fist clenched tightly around it. The weight at the end of the rope is feeling heavier now and the gondola is tipping under the strain as you hold onto the edge of the basket, still breathing hard.

The pilot looks at you compassionately and says "It's okay", you can let go of it now." She reaches for your hand that is still holding the rope.

"It's okay", she says again—just let it go… let it go." When you release the rope it quickly slips over the side and you catch a glimpse of the black ribbon with the red lettering and then you reach out for the pilot's hand— trusting that everything will be alright. The balloon rises quickly now—higher and higher and even higher. The balloon continues upward and you begin to be filled with the feeling of *Hopefulness* as the pilot navigates the balloon. Using all her skills the balloon moves up and into the clouds above a flock of geese. Looking down at the earth, now seeming further and further away—the pilot touches your shoulder and points upward.

When you look up you see that you are about to clear the atmosphere as blue sky is giving way to black and then—suddenly stars appear everywhere and seem almost close enough to touch!

"Are we in space?" you ask.

"Yes", the pilot answers with a twinkle in her eye.

"I'm feeling.... lighter and ...happier" you think to yourself. "Is this, the...universe?" you ask incredulously.

"Part of it", she replies.

"Which part—you ask as the balloon moves through the Milky Way—it is all so beautiful."

Then the pilot turns her eyes to meet yours and waves her arm around in a sweeping motion and says "this part is you" as she smiles even more brightly now and watches your reactions. Your heart leaps in your chest and you are filled with a deep sense of what can only be described as the feeling of pure *Love*. The feeling of *Love* is growing bigger as the balloon drifts slowly toward a beautiful golden platform.

The golden platform is lit-up with millions of beautiful brightly colored lights. The pilot skillfully lands the aircraft on the platform and you feel the basket come to a stop and the door on the basket opens up.

"We're here", the pilot points to the open door. Before stepping out you turn to the pilot and ask in wonderment, "where am I?" You feel the smile on your face as if you'd smiled for the first time.

With twinkling eyes she says "this is where all your wishes of Joy—Freedom—Love and Appreciation have all manifested and everything here and everyone here, has been waiting for you to show up."

"I'm not sure what you mean", you exclaim puzzled.

The pilot goes on to explain. "In your life there were many times you experienced things and people that you wished were different. When someone was rude to you, another part of you, a higher energy-level part of you wished they were not rude but more loving".

Continuing, she says, "When you felt discouraged because life was not turning out the way you had hoped and you felt sad or disappointed the higher energy-level part of you wished to be happy. All of these wishes from you, over the years, were like *bundles* of energy—that moved to this place. They have been kept here as they were wished for by you and then kept in a kind of *emotional escrow account*. This is the higher energy-level part of you—who and what you really are as a complete energy or divine being! In your essence— you are—pure Love and Joy. As you are able to *feel* feelings of Joy—Love and Appreciation, you will naturally be elevated to this place—and have access to all of this. But, should you *not allow* yourself to have these better-feeling emotions, then all of the ropes—get tied on again—and this place will become just a faint memory to you. It's time to go now" and she motions you to step out of the gondola —smiling warmly.

Stepping out of the basket, you notice that all of the colors on the platform seem to become brighter. There are beautiful sounds coming from everywhere—like choirs of angelic voices. A familiar figure is walking toward you. This being seems to be filled and surrounded with light and as they move closer—you recognize who they are—your heart flutters in your chest and tears of joy fill your eyes—this is someone you thought you would never see again and yet—here they are. Everywhere laughter and joyous sounds fill the air. Beautiful bright light is coming from everywhere. Now other beings are coming toward you and your heart fills and overflows with Joy as they approach.

Looking back at the pilot who is now standing at the door of the balloons gondola and waving goodbye to you—you excitedly shout out, "Am I in heaven?"

She laughs and shouts back to you. "Are you feeling Joy, Love and Appreciation for all that you have created?"

"Yes, yes, yes", you say.

"Then yes, you are in heaven."

"But, have I died?" you persist.

"No, you are just beginning to live". Looking at the gondola you notice for the first time—a brass sign with the name of the aircraft in black lettering—FORGIVENESS.

The pilot laughs as she fires the burners again and shouts out "heaven is—and always has been—a state of mind."

Guided Imagery

You can *fly* up the scale easily for a few minutes at a time if you use your imagination to create something beautiful. *The Balloon* is an imagery I created to speak to the Subconscious mind in symbols. Speaking of the lower emotional tones as weights (sandbags) that tie us down can be a powerful suggestion to our Subconscious mind to *let go* of the things (programs) that keep us away from experiencing all the higher emotional feelings of *Happiness* and *Love* that we all crave as human beings.

I have recorded *The Balloon guided imagery* with background theta music and nature sounds and it is available as a free MP3 download on my website. There are also other guided imagery recordings that have been written specifically for *the Mind Gate process*. Also, you have my permission to record this in your own voice for playback to yourself (as long as it is for your personal use) while playing theta brain wave meditation sounds or music while you are learning *the process*.

Visualizing images that evoke positive *emotional feelings* in you, even if they are general and without the expectation of receiving a specific item will be more effective in the long run, but sometimes we need to *prime the pump* of our imagination. I go over in detail what kinds of sounds and music that work best in Chapter 6: The Process— *Mind Gate Music*.

If you feel you are ready, then go ahead and begin using the process as outlined in Chapter 6. However, bear in mind that because we are often in a state of hypnosis — reading Chapter 7: How to De-hypnotize Ourselves can be of great value before beginning *the Mind Gate process*. There are basically two ways to recognize if you are in hypnosis during the so-called waking state.

1.) You will tend to *hang-out* frequently in the emotional tones below Hopefulness because—more likely than not—you are unable to focus your energy on thoughts or goals that would allow you to *experience* the higher tones.

2.) If you are feeling confused or overwhelmed quite often, know that you are escaping (fight or flight response) into hypnosis. This means that the *Critical area* or *Mind Gate* is *hemorrhaging* tons of message units into your Subconscious mind without being analyzed and then—all hell can break loose. You will need to learn how to *snap out of it* (waking hypnosis) as soon as possible. In other words— the gatekeeper is *asleep at the wheel* and you are *tranced.*

Confusion along with feelings of *being overwhelmed* are *red flags* to you and require immediate action— as soon as possible go straight to Chapter 7: How to Dehypnotize Ourselves. I know I am harping on this point but, you must realize that when you are tranced— you are attracting all manner of negative possibilities which— will eventually— take *form* and *manifest* as a reality in your world!

When you are in a waking state of hypnosis you have become a walking *time-bomb* and— when it goes off you could take others with you— so remember this. When our *mind gate* is *open* during our *waking hours* and left unattended by us (tranced) it will be nothing but trouble because—we are walking around in a hyper-suggestible state and literally anything (often negative message units) can drop down and stimulate our programs. Unfortunately the programs that usually get stimulated are the negative ones (70%).

So, unless you are at Disneyland and are in a *trance* of pure bliss— you are dangerous to yourself and those around you— so get out of hypnosis as soon as possible! In other words—wake up the gatekeeper!

This bears saying again. Get yourself out of hypnosis as soon as possible. When you are in a hyper- suggestible state and not directing what goes into the Subconscious mind, you are at the mercy of any and all negative influences— especially your own negative thoughts which may be running amuck. How will you know if your *negative* programs have been stimulated and are running, you may ask? Simple—ask your-self this—"how do I feel?"

In other words, what is your state of mind? Many bad real estate and automobile purchases have been made because we were in a state of hyper- suggestibility at the time of purchase. A good salesman knows just how far to push before you become confused and then more easily influenced by his words and gestures. They know about hyper-suggestibility.

I'm not picking on all salespeople here, only the unscrupulous ones. There are many honest and hardworking salespeople so don't let that stop you from purchasing what you want— just stay out of hypnosis when you do. Letting your-self go into hypnosis and not checking it— as soon as possible could be compared to leaving the barn door open and allowing all of your livestock to run away— or get attacked by hungry predators. So Chapter 7: How to De-Hypnotize Ourselves is a priority, a true *must-read*!

NOTE: If you live with other people or family then do your best to explain how this all works. Help them to stay out of hypnosis. Children get much better grades in school and have less behavioral issues when they are guided to stay out of hypnosis. You will help your children immeasurably by teaching them some of the principles in Chapter 7— and teach them about *the emotional tone scale.* You can read the rest of the book as you are practicing *the Mind Gate process.*

NOTE: Your First priority must always be to raise your emotional tone as quickly as possible because— that is *the key* to harnessing the power that creates your world— the power known as the law of attraction.

CHAPTER 6

The Process

"The mind is a superb instrument
if used correctly."
-The Power of Now

To get through the Mind Gate and impress an idea or thought of something you want, whether it be a material item, circumstance or just a pleasant *feel- good* scene onto or into the Subconscious mind— you have to *believe* you are worthy and have the right to do so. In order to believe you are worthy and have the right to do so— you must know *what* you are. In that knowing— you take full responsibility for all of your creations— in other words—the world you experience as your world! When you take *full* responsibility for *everything* you experience then you will then know *exactly* what to focus on and what *not* to focus on. If you are indeed the creator of your reality then why— oh why— would you want to create or *focus on* anything that does not feel good?

Jesus said this about the subject; "…turn the other cheek", in other words— turn your attention away from what you don't want to experience and— put your attention on what you do want to experience! This also applies to any negative thing or situation that has already become manifest or taken form in the *world*. Once it's been manifested or it is *in your face* as it t'were— then *stop looking at it*— turn away from it, or just plain ol'— ignore it! Begin thinking and putting your attention on what you really want! If there is a disaster in the world somewhere, it will do you and the victims no good whatsoever to talk about and stew about that disaster. I'm paraphrasing here—when Mother Teresa was asked if she would participate in a rally *against* the war she said "No, but if you give a rally *for* peace, I'll be there."

When a farmer plants a field he does not have thoughts or visions of the crop failing— and so it must be with you. You will be planting the seeds of *positive* feelings into your Subconscious mind. From this moment forward, commit yourself to the discipline of spending as little energy as absolutely necessary to attend to any negative situation that may have manifested and then— get out of there! This must become a way of life for you!

Intention

To get through the Mind Gate consciously and impress an idea or thought of something you want, whether it be a material item, circumstance or just— a pleasant "feel good" scene onto— or into the Subconscious mind you must first be clear about your **intention.** You must have the best intentions. Your intention can be just to *feel* better than you do right now. Whatever your intention and whatever it may be that you want— must also be good for others.

In other words, to get what you want should not mean that someone else cannot get what they want. This should never be about competition.... ever. *Feeling better* enriches not only *your* life but *all life!* This is the *ripple effect* or *butterfly effect*. The *butterfly effect* is a tenet of *chaos theory* that describes how— very small actions can have extremely large effects on complex systems. *Example: A butterfly flaps his wings in Peking and we get rain instead of snow in New York City.*

Your main intention should always be to raise your emotional tone —state of mind— vibration or energy! All of these words can be used interchangeably. So, your *intention* and number one priority must always be to *feel good.* What is— *feeling good*? Referring back to the emotional tone scale once more, we need to understand that any tone that is above where we are at any given moment is technically feeling good. Some might argue at this point and think —"How can feeling Rage be better than feeling Guilt?" Well, if you have ever felt severe Guilt then you know that Rage or Revenge feel a whole lot more powerful—or better than guilt—maybe even good!

It's as simple as that. Your state of mind, emotional tone, energy or vibration is **all that matters!** If you have a friend who is feeling down you will not help them by going down the scale to their state of mind. Have compassion but don't go down there with them. Do you save a drowning man by drowning yourself?

To get through the Mind Gate and impress an idea or thought of something you want, whether it be a material item, a positive circumstance or just a pleasant *feel-good* scene onto or into the Subconscious mind— you must first be conscious or consciously aware of why and what you are doing. The more you practice *the process* described here and visualize the desired condition (material item, positive circumstance or pleasant *feel-good* scene) the more it becomes your dominant thought or *suggestion* or *central idea* in your daily life— and through the law of attraction— your emotional tone or state of mind will act like a *powerful radio tower*— sending your *signal* out to attract to you— people, things and circumstances—that are *like* your *central idea, emotional tone* and *dominant thoughts.*

This is the all-powerful law of attraction which states— *every positive or negative event that happened with you was attracted by you.* The law of attraction responds in *like* fashion to your feelings. If you are feeling bad (like attracts like), that is what the *law of attraction* will send back to you— more *bad- feeling* reality. You could also think of the law of attraction like a mirror. If you are angry and yelling at yourself in a mirror, the image that is reflected back to you— is angry and yelling back at you. However, it would most probably serve you better to think of yourself as a giant radio transmitter.

Before you begin *the mind gate process*— I want you to be clear that you do not need *the process* to create your reality— you already do that. You need *the Mind Gate process* to create your *desired reality.* You are going to be creating *something* anyway— how good do you want your life to be?

THE PROCESS

At night before bed or shortly after awakening or anytime during the day when you can be reasonably certain you will not be disturbed, sit back in a semi-reclined position in bed, recliner chair or even upright in a comfortable chair.

Uncross your hands and feet and make sure your neck and head are supported comfortably. The reason to be semi-reclined is so you can breathe more deeply into the lower abdomen.

Make sure your telephone is on silent or is turned off. If you own a cat, a dog or any other pets, be sure to have them in another room or somewhere where they cannot disturb you. This is absolutely vital to your success.

A darkened room is best but you may use an eye mask if you'd like. If you have an iPod, CD player or even your computer to play your meditation music, that's fine but— it is best if you use headphones or properly fitting ear buds. The reason for this is, there is more of a noise barrier produced with headphones.

When you begin to pass through the Mind Gate to be conscious in the Subconscious mind you will be entering into what Eckhard Tolle calls *the Now* or *Presence*— and it is silent which is in stark contrast to your conscious mind.

The music will keep your *monkey mind* entertained. The *monkey mind* will become bored eventually and stop its chatter. In hypnotherapy we call this— going into *abeyance*. The background music, beats or noise should be chosen carefully. Some people use sound machines. Sound machines with nature sounds like Ocean, Meadow sounds, Streams, Heartbeat and Rain are best if you choose to use these.

While sound machines are good, I have found what works best is to use music that has been developed for meditation purposes and help the body and mind calm down so it moves more easily into the slower brain-wave patterns of Alpha or Theta.

If you are very tired you may slip into deep sleep while doing *the process*. This is okay if you can get in at least ten to fifteen minutes of positive visualization and *feel-good* emotions before drifting off to delta (unconscious) sleep. Hypnosis or the alpha and theta brain-waves are also known as the *creative* states.

If falling asleep after your session appeals to you then put your iPod, iTunes or CD player on *Repeat* or (endless loop) so you can drift off to sleep after your visualization. Initially, I would suggest you use *the process* both— before sleep and upon awakening. To create the life you want, I think thirty minutes a day (fifteen minutes in the morning and fifteen minutes before sleep) is well worth the time spent and should not be a hardship— and because it feels so good— you'll look forward to your next session.

If you do *the process* during the day or anytime you have to be somewhere, please use a timer to wake you in fifteen to twenty minutes. It is so easy to stay in the deeper states because we are more fully relaxed than we are in our normal *waking* or beta brain wave state and oftentimes two or more hours can pass and feel like— only minutes. The more real you make your visualizations, the longer you will tend to stay in the deeper states.

If you are fairly new to meditation, I would recommend you use a timer anyway. The reason for this is two-fold: *The Mind Gate process* utilizes extremely powerful induction techniques that are designed to bring you into a very deep state of relaxation or trance, so you may fall asleep, especially if you are very tired. And if that part of you (your Conscious mind) that is focusing on some beautiful scene knows it only has to do this for a short amount of time— there will be less resistance from your *monkey mind*— so there will be less chance of it drawing your attention away to something unwanted or some concern you may have— so why paddle upstream? Our *monkey mind* is very clever, so the sooner we learn to *observe it* without getting sucked into its *thought-stream,* the better off we will be!

If some W*orry or Fear—creeps* into your consciousness and you find that you can't seem to *focus* back— to your visualization then put your attention immediately onto your *energy field* —that you can feel in your feet or hands. It will be that slight vibratory or subtle tingling sensation deep in the body. Then, breathe deeply again into the lower stomach. This will help you *snap back* into present time— and then, reconnect to your body.

Breathing

When you are ready— with yourself in position and your music playing loud enough to buffer most street noise or other noises—begin breathing deep into the diaphragm. This is accomplished by pretending there is a balloon in your lower stomach or waist. Some call this *yoga- breathing* —but professional singers learn how to breathe this way also. As you breathe deeply into the abdomen— you are taking in more oxygen and breathing out carbon dioxide which activates the para-sympathetic nervous system.

This is the part of the nervous system that calms us down. Continue breathing in this manner for about five minutes, allowing yourself to hold your breath in for a moment or two before exhaling and—eventually— begin breathing out a little more slowly than you breathe in.

Visualize

After about 5 minutes of yoga-breathing— allow your mind to visualize, imagine or pretend that you are thoroughly enjoying a cherished goal that you have longed for. It could be a new house, career, vacation, relationship or anything that *feels good* when you imagine having it— manifest.

Let yourself go— anywhere that feels good to you. There should be nothing but pleasant feelings when you do this. If you can't think of, or are not ready to go for a specific goal yet, that's okay! Remember...the purpose and *intention* here is to *feel good!* This is all about raising your emotional tone— energy and vibration —so just visualize, imagine or pretend *anything* that *feels good!*

Or maybe, you can see yourself— in a cottage by the ocean, or in the woods —or by a stream— playing an instrument or singing. Perhaps you see yourself— speaking in front of an audience and hear them clapping and giving you a standing ovation. Or maybe, you are flying over a beautiful countryside.

It's your vision and it doesn't have to be work. In fact, this is really play, *but* make no mistake —*the process* will attract all the good stuff to you— no matter what the vision is—because, as your Subconscious gets the message that you are *feeling good* it will then *act* on those feelings— by attracting *more* of what *feels- good* into your physical reality. So, go easy with this. It's all about *being happy* for a few minutes— consistently— *on the other side* of the Mind

Gate— because— you are now *deliberately* creating that happiness!

Anchor

As soon as you begin to feel a *good feeling* with your visualization or imagining put your left index finger and thumb together as if you are making an OK sign. This *anchors* or locks-in that thought, picture or visualization into the good feeling. (Remember the Balloon guided imagery) Then— use your new *anchor* to get that picture and feeling many times throughout your day. An *anchor* is like a muscle, the more you use it, the stronger it becomes— and the more effective it becomes. The big idea here is to remind yourself of that *good-feeling* thought— as often as possible until— it becomes automatic. This is a great way to affect your state-of-mind.

If you are having difficulty visualizing at first then, while you are breathing deeply, put your mental attention on your feet or hands until you feel a little tingling, buzzing or even a pleasant numbing sensation in the feet or hands. Then practice changing the temperature from cold to warm and back again in your hands or feet. What you are feeling is your body's energy field. It is very subtle so if you have to pretend or imagine it at first that is okay. Tuning into your body in this manner helps you to get into and stay in *present time* or the NOW as Eckhart Tolle says. This feels so amazing and absolutely wonderful that this is a meditation in and of itself. Use your body's deep subtle feelings whenever you begin to be distracted. You may even want to start with going deep into the body and even stay there until you get comfortable doing the process.

Another great way to stimulate the imagination is this. While listening to your music— imagine or pretend you are listening to the musician playing live for you. What instrument are they playing? Are they in a concert hall or club and —what do they look like? Are they male or female? Another way to stimulate the imagination if you are listening to ocean surf or wind is to pretend you can feel the wind against your face or pretend you can smell the ocean. If you are listening to meadow sounds then maybe pretend you can feel a gentle breeze in the meadow and listen to hear any meadow sounds like birds—where are they? What kind of bird do you think they may be—and what do they look like?

It doesn't matter if you can actually see or visualize a scene or not. If you can *feel* your body you can do this. Pictures will come to you eventually so don't be disturbed or let that stop you from doing *the Mind Gate process.* Persist, as if your life depended on it because your happiness and satisfaction in life (and probably many others) is dependent upon your being able to raise your emotional tone and state of mind!

> "Whenever an answer, a solution, or a creative idea is needed, stop thinking for a moment by focusing your attention on your inner energy field. Become aware of the stillness." –Eckhart Tolle

Discipline yourself to keep coming back to your visualization or to the good feeling when any negative or *to do* thought tries to creep into your meditation. This includes body discomforts. It is okay to scratch an itch but your monkey mind is clever and doesn't want to give up control. It may try to distract you in a number of ways. If you persist it will eventually quiet down as you notice its antics for what they are. However, when it does *act up* again later— remember to *observe* it as if it were a small child tugging at your coat or—even throwing a *temper tantrum*. There will be other times that *it* will be quite convincing that *it*— is you!

It can even use Fear or Worry programs to grab your attention but eventually you will come to realize that it is *You* who are in control and then— *it* will have little effect on your state of mind, if any. It is critical that you understand this not only for manifesting good stuff but— for your own peace of mind. There is *nothing,* and I do mean *nothing* that is more important than you learning and practicing how to *feel good!*

Raising your emotional tone will not only attract more *like* things (good stuff) to you but will also direct your attention— during waking hours to—people, places and things that will bring you more of what you want. Opportunity will show up or you will become aware of it where— in the past— you may have never even noticed it—even if it were right in front of you.

It's perfectly okay and even normal that as you practice your visualization may change—it may become more detailed or less detailed. You are going for *feelings* here so allow your visualizations to go anywhere that *feels* good to you. Your meditations and visualizations will begin to incorporate more and more of the five senses as they evolve and change. So it's okay as you practice *the process* to let your *feelings* guide you, just so long as they are guiding you to better-feeling thoughts or picture and into the higher emotional tones. You will soon gain a feel for *the process* so remember— this is a *skill* you are learning. Just go easy and have fun with this but continue to practice— practice— practice! It will all come easily to you very soon.

Always remember that it is you who is creating the visualization—if you don't like it—then you can change it. You are the writer, director and producer— so make it just as wonderful, kooky, crazy, zany or beautiful as you like. Again, just have fun with this and remember it is perfectly okay if it begins to feel or seems as if you are just *goofing off.* In fact, that's one of the biggest validations or affirmations that you are on the right track and moving forward in the right direction. Moving toward Joy always feels a little like goofing off.

When it becomes more and more like play-time you are there—you are *in the zone* so get ready to receive your *good stuff.* Keeping your visualizations more general is extremely productive so don't get *bummed* if you can't seem to come up with a specific goal or desire. Remember, you have a *huge* positive *emotional escrow account* that's just sitting there and waiting for you to *show up* on its frequency or tone!

> "Your father in heaven knows what you need before you ask…." -Jesus

Do not let any negative (lower emotional tone feelings) creep into your process time. This is your work here. You will soon become very good at knowing how to switch back quickly to *good-feeling* pictures and thoughts. I cannot stress this enough! You must learn to ignore the *monkey mind*—by just noticing when it comes around— and then re-redirect your conscious attention back to your *good-feeling* visualization. This is how you train your mind to focus.

Monkey Mind

Do not under any circumstances engage the *monkey mind*. Let me be very clear about this. Would you get in between two Grizzly bears fighting? It would be futile and you would likely get badly injured. That's how I want you think of your *monkey mind*. Your *monkey mind* does not care about your welfare. It does not care if you are happy. It is afraid you may wake up and realize that it is not the real you. It wants control of your mind. It would even kill you if it could figure out a way to do it without dying itself! Observe it from a distance. You must always be the observer and never let yourself be fooled again. The *monkey mind*— disguising itself as your thoughts— is simply negative programs running— and that is all. You must remember this always! It is not real, no matter how real it may seem and— even if you *are* experiencing a *negative* life situation that it wants you to put your attention on— you will not improve that situation by *thinking* about it.

Your Conscious mind is way out of practice at fantasizing so it will want to figure things out. That is what you believe you are supposed to do and the monkey mind loves to engage the Conscious mind in figuring stuff out but you have forgotten how to use the Conscious mind properly. You have forgotten how to focus on what you want. Remember, you are the director and producer of your life movie and that is what your Conscious mind is designed to do.

That's What I'm Talkin' About

Once you have unwittingly created a negative reality or negative manifestation it has already gained way too much momentum to *figure it out* anyway because— it has already been created. You cannot *un-create* it but it will eventually lose steam and peter-out on its own like a hurricane— and go away if your conscious attention is drawn away from it— and onto a more positive reality or something you really want—so always remember to "…turn the other cheek". Am I saying you should ignore the reality of a negative situation? Yes and no. The best you can do is to take responsibility for your creation by saying something like; "Look what I created!"

In other words, acknowledge it as your creation and then turn away from it and go back to the drawing board. Turn your conscious attention and use your imagination to create something you really want. Now, by the same token, go ahead and *take credit* for any *good* situation in the same manner. In fact, I highly recommend you do just that! Saying "Look what I created!" is a wonderful affirmation for knowing *what* ou really are! Or, a wonderful thing that I have been saying to myself lately when I experience something that is pleasing to me is "That's what I'm talkin' about!" or simply— TWITA! I got that from a good friend of mine and his grandson. Or you could say, "That's more like it!" Anything that affirms *anything* that is pleasing to you— and shows up in your life as good— is worth acknowledging. It could be as simple as feeling Appreciation and gratitude for having eyesight to read this book! This moves you into an emotional tone of Appreciation. "Yeah, baby, that's what I'm talkin' about" My wife just made a yummy protein drink. "TWITA!"

Commitment

In order to get results and get what you want you must—commit to doing *the Mind Gate Process* for at least fifteen minutes each day— no matter what! Soon you will be able to direct your attention back to your visualization during your day to day life. At first you will be using your *anchor* and then one day— your entire life will be transformed as you visualized it to be—or even better. How long will it take to get results? The magic number is twenty one days to see definite changes in your time-space reality. In the meantime— just notice what you have created so far and take credit (not blame) for all of it.

By the same token, do not give credit nor blame to anyone or anything else because that is the path to *Disempowerment*.

As Yoda said in Star Wars, "Fear is the path to the dark side". When we blame others for something negative in our life or give them credit for something good we are affirming— on a very deep level that we do not create our own life— and this puts us into fear. We feel we are at the mercy of fate or the economy or something. It is okay to feel *Empowered* because you are a God among Gods but you are not more than— nor less than—anyone—anywhere.

When we can express gratitude for anything we experience, whether it appears as good or bad and remember that we are the creators of it we are acknowledging who and what we really are which is the feeling of *Appreciation*. Look at all the good in your life and remember to always thank your-self for it because— you deserve all the credit for all the good that is around you!

We must always keep in mind—that negative circumstances will not change—until we change how we feel.

We must plant our seeds of happiness in the only place where they can grow and that is deep in our subconscious mind. Then, we must tend our garden by watering and nurturing them, keeping the weeds out all the while.

Mind Gate Music

I have experimented with this extensively and have found that synthesizer music by artists like Steven Halpern, Dan Gibson, Ty Burhoe and others combined with ocean surf sounds, streams, rivers or rain work better to engage our *monkey mind.*

As that part of the mind becomes distracted, you will be able to drift into a relaxed *alpha* or *theta* state more rapidly and be able stay in those states for longer periods of time. Nature sounds in the background provide a kind of *white noise* and aid to help keep us focused on our visualizations. A company called "Hemi-Sync" (go to www.hemisync.com) has a lot of "Brainwave" CD's available for meditation. Listen to their samples first— to *feel* if it resonates with you— given my criteria of checking with how it *feels* to you on the emotional tone scale.

I personally like combining various types of *meditation music* with nature sounds. I have CD's and MP3's on my website that are especially powerful as meditation tools. Check out "Sublime Sea" and "Transcendent River" that are available for download on our website. These recordings have been specially arranged for use with *the Mind Gate process,* guided imagery and self-hypnosis.

The Balloon is also available as a narrated guided imagery fantasy with special *theta brain wave* music composed, arranged and recorded by Kim Nejak to go along with the story and is an incredible audio-visual odyssey. It is what I like to call *mind candy*.

The Mind Gate process is also available in a narrated format as a progressive relaxation to guide you through *the process* with *alpha* and *theta* brain wave and *binaural* beats that help you reach even deeper states of *theta* brain wave states. After the narrated *progressive relaxation* that incorporates extremely powerful *positive suggestions* that help you visualize and experience feelings at the highest levels of the emotional tone scale— the music continues for an hour— so you can fall asleep to it if you'd like.

NOTE: Do not play Rock, Rap, Jazz or anything that will excite you. Music that has melodies from songs you know— or music with words does not work because it will distract you from your visualization and it can—get the *monkey mind* chattering so much that you won't be able to focus—on the silence— deep within you.

Chapter 7

How to De-Hypnotize Ourselves

"Within each of us is a light, awake..."
-Tony Samara

Looking back now I realize that, for the most part— during times of great stress— I was in a state of hypnosis—in the *fight or flight response.* So, if you haven't guessed it by now, you are probably running around, for the most part, in a state of hypnosis yourself— and so is nearly everyone you know. I know you probably don't want to hear that but "facts is facts"! As most of my colleagues in hypnotherapy can tell you, our clients are already in hypnosis when they come to see us the first time— and we have to de-hypnotize them before we can hypnotize them.

Why? In Chapter 3: The Mind Gate, I illustrate how the mind works. I outline the mechanism of *fight or flight* and— how our Conscious mind *escapes* into hypnosis— a simulated sleep or trance state from—an overload of *message units* (too many mind). When we were *cave-people*, sitting around our *cave- fire* and cooking *woolly mammoth* steaks on a spit— when suddenly a saber-toothed tiger—decided to join us for dinner— we had to be able to fight or run away... really fast!

We still have those reactions and, in fact, we experience them quite often—some days numerous times. It is known as the fight or flight response. Our heart beats faster and our breathing rate increases as adrenaline is pumped into our blood stream.

The fight or flight response is a function of our *sympathetic nervous system* as opposed to our parasympathetic nervous system which is the part of our nervous system that relaxes and calms us down. The fight or flight response was necessary for survival in *cave-people* days but is rarely essential for survival in today's world because there aren't any more saber-toothed tigers around anymore these days but—our ancestors didn't have freeways with seventy mile per hour traffic to deal with. Our fight or flight response was not stimulated on a regular basis as cave-people and—we had time to recover from such reactions.

Today, between the internet, television, commuter traffic, school activities for our kids, insurance issues, economy unknowns and aging parents— we don't have much recovery time. I know, we get recovery time— it's called a vacation. However, no matter how much time we get for vacation—it's not enough time to offset the routine assault we tolerate to our bodies and minds from regular *fight or flight* responses in our everyday lives. And even worse, many find their vacations so overwhelming and stressful that— they are in hypnosis through most of it.

This is why it can feel like our vacations are over just as we were starting to unwind. These feelings of *overwhelm* or *information overload* cause the fight or flight response to be triggered and—we escape into a state of hypnosis or trance. We become *hyper-suggestible* to any negativity in our environment— including our own negative thoughts.

Being in hypnosis during waking hours is probably the biggest cause of a negative state of mind or low emotional tone there is. People rarely if ever get overloaded or *stressed-out* by having too many positive message units! There may be exceptions to this I suppose, like teenagers who may be *in-love*. And no, you don't have to be a teenager to be *in-love* but— when we are bombarded with information on a daily basis that is coming from the environment, other people, situations and activities— if we don't plan ahead— we can easily go into hypnosis.

Just think about how much information you receive and are subjected to every day. For example; let's start with *waking- up* to an alarm clock— informing us— or giving us information about— what time it is. As we go through our morning routine to get ready for our day, we may have to go to the bathroom, get a cup of coffee or make a cup of tea. We may check our telephone for voicemails or emails and text messages, look at Facebook—take a shower, pick out our clothes to wear today, put on our makeup, get dressed, go back to the kitchen— fix ourselves some breakfast (if we even eat breakfast), eat our breakfast or wrap it up to go, put on our coat, grab our car keys and briefcase then— head out the door. We may drive whatever distance we drive to work or— walk to the bus stop, encounter other people commuting, negotiate traffic and listen to the radio news or a motivational CD and then arriving at work, parking the car or stepping off the bus with the morning newspaper under our arm after having read it on the bus or train with the latest *upsetting news* before finally— settling into our work- routine for the day. And I didn't even touch on all the other possible stimulation —partners, kids, pets, etc.

We are receiving a whole lot of information before we even start our workday. In addition to all this information coming to us— through our eyes, ears, nose, mouth and skin— there is also a voluminous amount of information coming into our *conscious* awareness from our physical bodies. For example; the meal we had last night may not be settling very well in our stomach and we may notice we are uncomfortable—somewhere. If that is not enough, our Subconscious mind may be reacting to the events that occurred the day before and sending us an incredible amount of messages as *emotions.* "What did he mean when he said / she said_____?"

These feelings or emotions may or may not be pleasant and so we try to analyze where they are coming from. According to Dr. John Kappas; "A hyper-suggestible individual is in a waking 'trance-state 'and can easily be affected by negative influences in the environment… hyper -suggestibility then, is a state in which the individual consciously responds… in the same way that he would respond to stimuli in the hypnotic state. When a person is in the hypnotic state [as when they are under hypnosis in the hypnotists' office], his receptiveness to what he experiences, through his senses, is intensified."

So, you need to accept that you are probably in a state of hypnosis most of the time and— it is pointless to put up an argument to the contrary because— it does not serve us to argue this point. With as much as we are exposed to on a daily basis, not even to mention all the information coming into our conscious awareness from our so-called *thoughts*— how often do you think you are not hypnotized? That is to say—how much of what you experience is *real* reality? Probably *not much because* neuropsychologists estimate that at best it's only about maybe five percent. So, in order to experience more *real* reality, it would be desirable— to be *awake!*

Move Your Body

Let's *wake-up* a moment— shall we? Reach your hands up toward the sky (or ceiling) and stretch...then move your stretched arms to one side and then the other. Do this three to five times so you can feel a really good stretch. If you'd like, at the same time— you can think about anything that feels good. Thoughts like— *how great it is that I am learning this* or— perhaps something you are excited about or grateful for are all really good thoughts. They could be something that really turns you on— or just feel your body for a few moments— whatever feels good to you is okay— just as long as you move. It doesn't really matter. You can stretch and make *goofy faces* in the mirror (my personal favorite).

I was at a seminar once and the speaker said he likes to start his day off with a laugh. His morning routine before showering was to jump up and down on a mini trampoline to the theme song from "Rocky III"— the "Eye of the Tiger" wearing nothing except his black ten-gallon Stetson cowboy hat in front of a full length mirror. The point is to move your body to get the energy moving, especially stuck *negative* emotional energy! Laughing at ourselves is an amazing way to move the negative energy out of our bodies and mind. "Eye of the Tiger"—what a great way to start the day!

"Everything is energy, that's all there is to it...".- Albert Einstein

Moving your body (changing your physiology) and thinking a *better-feeling* thought is the fastest and easiest way to *de-hypnotize* yourself— if —you are not in too deep. If you are really tranced then you'll probably forget to do this. It's all just vigilance—just being aware. You cannot afford to be *tranced* when you may be exposed to *negative* elements and this is fairly easy to do. If you are in the car and in *commuter* traffic, instead of listening to the radio or music—when you are stopped— make funny faces in your rear-view mirror or shrug your shoulders or both at the same time for a minute or so. If you notice other drivers looking at you— just smile. Who cares what they think? You will be *awake.*

Count Yourself Out

Another way to come out of the tranced state is to *count your-self out* of hypnosis— like I do, when finishing up a hypnotherapy session with a client.

Any time you are feeling overwhelmed or confused say to yourself or out loud, "ONE, TWO, THREE. FOUR, FIVE...EYES OPEN AND WIDE AWAKE...ONE, TWO, THREE, FOUR, FIVE...EYES OPEN AND WIDE AWAKE! Remember to say this TWO TIMES! Then, *breathe in* very deeply and hold it for a moment—then *breathe out* a little more slowly than you *breathed in* for five or six times.

A Breath of Fresh Air

When we are stressed, we often forget to breathe in deeply. Instead we do faster *shallow* breathing to get ready for *fight or flight.* When we are babies we naturally breathe into our stomachs and sometime along the way we quit breathing that way. We *learn* how to breathe shallow. If you stand up and hold one hand on your chest and the other hand on your lower abdomen and breathe a few *regular* breaths and then notice— which hand moves the most. Most likely, you will notice the movement under your hand that is over your chest is moving more than the one that is over your lower abdomen.

We learn to breathe shallow from an early age because when we are stressed— our *fight or flight* response becomes stimulated. Our breath becomes more rapid and shallow to get us ready to fight or run (remember our cave-people days?). Unfortunately— in our stress-filled society, we get into a habit of breathing this way and so— it seems normal to us. Taking five minutes —three times per day to lie down or even stand up—breathe in deeply into your lower stomach as if you are inflating a balloon—you will activate your parasympathetic nerve system—which will then activates our *relaxation response.*

Many people have a difficult time with this, so instead of *imagining* that you are inflating a balloon in your lower stomach— try letting your back, rib cage and lower stomach muscles go limp as you breathe in. This usually releases some of the chronic tension long enough for you to get the idea. It will feel strange to you at first but— it works beautifully to restore your body— and your mind to a more relaxed state and at the same time— pulling you effectively—out of hypnosis.

Eat to Prevent Anxiety and Hypnosis

Okay, so how or when should I use these techniques, you may ask? Wherever and whenever you feel *stressed beyond reason*! So, what is *beyond reason*— you may be thinking? As I said before— you will feel *overwhelmed, overloaded* or *confused.* You'll probably know but, if by some chance you don't, then you may know by the signs and symptoms of extreme stress— if you are aware. Unfortunately, we often don't realize we have been *stressed- out* until later, when we reflect back. Anyway, here are the symptoms: Rapid pulse, shortness of breath, nausea, lightheadedness, confusion, difficulty making decisions, etc. In short— you are having a mild to moderate panic-attack. Of course, we rarely acknowledge that is what we are having— unless it is severe.

We cannot function as a *fully-awake* human being if our brain is in panic-mode a much of the time. Now, you may not know this, but our brains— use a lot of energy and— this energy comes from glucose or *blood sugar. Blood sugar* comes from the food we eat. The *best* food to maintain a steady supply of *blood sugar* to the brain and— for the longest period of time is— protein. When we go too long without a steady supply of blood sugar (over 3-4 hours) from protein, our brain will begin to panic and send messages to the pancreas to slow down metabolism to conserve the energy needs of the body so we begin to feel tired or release insulin thereby giving us hypoglycemia (low blood sugar).

Our adrenal glands then react by releasing adrenalin to boost our energy and to tell us to *get up and find some food.* This triggers a *fight or flight response* in the sympathetic nervous system. We may get a little nervous and jittery as if we've had too much caffeine and our blood pressure rises. The adrenal glands signal the pancreas to raise the blood sugar but if there's no fuel available our blood sugar continues to drop and we go into a sort of insulin shock. We become confused and look for any source of blood sugar we can. We can get cranky and become *zoned- out.* In other words, we escape into hypnosis to deal with the bio-chemical stress to the brain. The bottom- line here, if you eat some protein— four ounces or about one half cup— or more if you do heavy physical work— you will be giving your brain what it needs and it is less likely to go into *panic-mode.*

I am asked frequently, "What is protein?" or "What are examples of protein?" Before I answer that, let me tell you why protein at regular intervals works. Proteins take longer to break down and be converted into blood sugar than carbohydrates and therefore supply a more steady supply of glucose to the brain and body. Long before we had grocery stores and *fast- foods*, we were hunters and gatherers. *Paleolithic Man* (Old Stone Age 4.5 million years ago), also known as *homo erectus,* were probably our (*homo sapiens*) ancestors. They were very successful for millions of years.

They hunted meat, fish, reptiles and all sorts of other forms of protein that I am sure, you would not be too interested in eating today. They grazed throughout the day living on wild plants, fruits and pieces of protein from earlier kills. When their *fight or flight response* was triggered —they needed to have all their wits about them to survive— hunt and gather another day.

(see "The Paleo Diet" by Loren Cordain, PH.D.)

Modern humans are now so used to this *fight or flight response* (information overload) happening that we are in a frequent state of hypnosis (remember we escape by going into a simulated sleep and sometimes fight) when we are under a lot of stress. The longer we are exposed to stress (chronic stress) the easier we go into hypnosis. We have become desensitized and have even learned to *turn-off* our brains normal signal to eat— so many times— we often forget to eat.

So— what is stress? It's different for everyone depending on our Subconscious programs— with some exceptions but— if you catch yourself *zoning- out* or *worrying* about things you can't really control then— it's a safe bet to say— you are stressed.

Stress takes its toll— not only our body— but on our minds as well. After years of stressful situations, we eventually become *desensitized* to it and *numb-out* in one way or another as a way to cope. We overreact to people and situations because our brain or mind is already *disorganized* and confused.

If you or anyone you know matches these descriptions then— you or they— are in hypnosis or tranced a lot of the time.

So, what are some good sources of protein? Since we have lost many of our *hunter-gatherer* skills— over the ages and— have gotten used to our domestic diet— we have to learn a whole new way of eating. Here's a partial list. You may have to become creative and/or plan ahead to have *protein snacks* available. Now, I am not saying eat protein only because— we need all of the minerals and vitamins that we get from fresh fruits and vegetables (I prefer organic everything).

Please check your library or the internet for a complete list and meal planning ideas. If you don't like to cook— you can still do this. My website has a Food Guide that you can read and download for free. www.DrMitchellMays.com

It is important to understand that *you must feed your brain* regularly with quality food to help it function optimally. I highly recommend "The Paleo Diet by Dr. Loren Cordain. His book has been highly researched and puts it all together for you. But if you would like a *quick- start* guide to get you by for now, the following list may be helpful:

Meats, seafood, fish and fowl are excellent sources of animal protein.

Dairy Products, Eggs

Cottage cheese, pot cheese, Farmer's cheese, all crane cheeses, hard cheeses, Kiefer, acidophilus milk, Greek yogurt (without honey or sugar is better), butter.

Hard cheeses contain twice the amount of protein of most soft cheeses.

Nuts, Seeds & Grains are excellent vegetarian sources of complete proteins

Raw pine nuts, butter nuts, Brazil nuts, pumpkin and squash seeds, walnuts, pecans, almonds, peanuts, sesame seeds and flax seeds. Hemp seeds are now becoming more readily available and are an excellent source of protein.

Raw almonds are my personal favorite.

Ancient whole grains (non-GMO)

Brown Rice, Millet, Quinoa, oats, barley, rye, buckwheat

Nut Butters and Tahini (sesame butter) are good sources of protein and can be used for snacks but read labels to make sure no sugar has been added, especially corn syrup. If a product has sugar, make sure it is cane sugar or fruit sugar. If you are diabetic or severely hypoglycemic then you must be suspect of all added sugars. So, read labels carefully.

Snacks

Snacks should be eaten every 2 to 3 hours and must consist of protein. A serving should be one quarter to one half cup. Snacks are to be eaten between meals, however if a meal is delayed an additional snack should be eaten. Also remember to eat a protein snack before bedtime regardless if you had ice cream for dessert or I should say, especially if you had a sugary desert.

Nuts or seeds, cooked cereal left over from breakfast, one half Apple and a few slices of cheese, raw vegetables and cream cheese, hard-boiled egg, deviled egg, leftover meat (three small slices), shrimp cocktail, Greek yogurt (unsweetened) with vegetable or fruit, peanut butter with whole grain crackers, fruit, or celery sticks.

If you did nothing else but eat *some* protein (four to six ounces) every three hours it would probably be enough to keep you out of hypnosis all day. In addition, your overall stress reactions to *negative* life situations would diminish greatly and— your emotional tone would climb naturally up the scale. Your state of mind would also improve. Have you ever noticed how *grouchy* people can get when they've gone too long without eating— especially men?

One of the greatest problems with today's teenagers, and I'm not picking on them, is their diet. Younger children, for the most part have serious *attention deficit* problems and— most would be helped easily by— making sure they get regular protein and— NOT sugar— for God's sake! Giving candy to children to shut them up or— as a reward is asking for big trouble later because children under eight or nine years of age are already in the hypnotic state and— you will program their Subconscious mind to go for sweets when they feel cranky or stressed in the future. Give them a protein snack instead.

With that said, your own diet probably needs improvement. I've had many clients tell me they eat very well. Many tell me they don't eat junk food— which is good but— they often go far too many hours without eating protein. They think that a piece of fruit in mid-afternoon will sustain them enough to last to dinner and pass as a healthy diet. Remember, when we go into hypnosis during our waking hours we become a little *fuzzy-thinking* and have *confusion* of thought due to the Mind Gate disorganizing. Our sympathetic nervous system has already been triggered and put us into *fight or flight* and— we go into hypnosis and become tranced. We, of course think nothing of it. It's just *normal* to us because almost everyone else is tranced too!

There's an old saying that goes like this: *It's hard to think about draining the swamp when you're up to your ass in alligators.*

That describes a lot of the behavior we encounter on a regular basis, not only from ourselves but others as well. Eating protein every three hours is something you can actually plan, however, it is nearly impossible to plan how to react to a stressful situation that seemingly *comes out of the blue!* I would encourage you to start *the Mind Gate process* along with changing your diet. It only takes a little bit of planning but it would give you a jump-start to manifesting a higher emotional tone so— rather than starting from F*ear, Insecurity* or A*nger*— you could start much higher up the scale just from eating protein every three hours! I strongly encourage you to share this information with your family, friends and co-workers as—this little bit of information alone will— make a huge difference in their lives and yours.

It will take three or four weeks for your brain's chemistry to settle-down and begin to trust you to provide regular quality fuel. I have witnessed many people's lives turn around completely in as little as— one week— just by learning how to breathe and eat protein every three hours. If you have children who have any learning challenges whatsoever, just by having them do these two things alone can make all the difference.

Don't worry about gaining weight— because, after your body and your brain chemistries begin to normalize, you will lose anything (and probably more) that you may have gained, and anyway, it's not usually more than two to three pounds. If you are underweight however, you may not lose the small weight-gain but— you will be much healthier.

A Word About Water

I know, I know, you've heard it a million times, "you need to drink more good water". So, let me just say this— about that. Coffee and other caffeinated beverages do not substitute for water, in fact, they are diuretics so— if you indulge in a lot of coffee because, it *wakes you up* (I'm sorry if I burst your bubble) you need to know that coffee stimulates the adrenal glands— which trigger the sympathetic nervous system and cause the *fight or flight response* so— instead of a triple-shot café mocha (oh my God) try a fruit smoothie with protein.

There are several *juice bars* around now that cater to *healthy-minded* individuals and— they even have coffee-flavored protein meal replacement smoothies! Beer is not a good substitute for water— even though it is mostly water. The alcohol will dehydrate you and it can make you very relaxed. Two beers will lower your brain waves down into alpha or even the theta state (hello, hypnosis).

Remember hyper- suggestibility? If you are going to drink alcohol, make sure you have been keeping your emotional tone up as high as possible. Do not drink too much alcohol if you are in a very bad state of mind because it will create an even worse one. If you are serious about how you feel and what you want to attract into your life then— at the very least— cut back on the caffeine some. Instead, if you have to, order your café mocha with only one shot. I promise you that your adrenal glands and brain will be happier and— a whole lot calmer.

If you absolutely cannot drink *plain* water or bottled water then I suggest you go to a *health food* store or go online and get "SweetLeaf" flavored liquid stevia drops. These are like- totally good for you—are all natural and flavor your water deliciously and beautifully. My favorite is Chocolate Raspberry, "yummy!" They come in a variety of flavors: Apricot Nectar, Grape, Root Beer, Chocolate, Cinnamon, English Toffee, Hazelnut, Peppermint, Lemon drop, Valencia Orange, Vanilla Crème, etc. These can also be substituted for sugar in the kitchen since— you are getting so healthy now. They are 100% natural, low calories, no carbohydrate and no glycemic. These can be used in smoothies, coffee, yogurt, whipped cream and anything else that you would like to sweeten. It's great for dieting and getting in more water but not as a substitute for protein!

I had written earlier that I believe many *attention deficit* diagnoses are simply a matter of the individual being in hypnosis much of the day. Attention deficit disorder responds very well to the three hour protein food plan. If you want to take this to the next higher level then switch to organic foods whenever possible. There is a plethora of information and research available on the Internet about protein and organic foods and their positive effect on attention deficit disorder in children and adults. Attention deficit is a matter of being unable to focus on a task and is, in my opinion the result, in most cases of *disorganization* of the critical area or Mind Gate, i.e. waking- hypnosis or trance state.

Once again, I cannot stress enough how important it is to *stay out of hypnosis* during our so-called *waking hours* unless you are doing *the process*. Allowing your-self to go into hypnosis without controlling it is tantamount to a Boeing 747 on autopilot. Eventually it will crash and when it does— it will take all of its passengers down with it. At the very least, it's "like giving a hammer to a four-year-old".

If you have a smart phone, you can program it to notify you every three hours to remind you to eat protein. You can also program it or download apps that remind you to *breathe deeply into the stomach for five minutes three times a day*. You can also use a simple digital timer and clip it to your belt or purse if you don't mind the annoying little "beep, beep, beep". Actually, that may start to make you salivate and restore your hunger signals, so go ahead, get the annoying kitchen timer. Whatever you have to do to keep yourself in *present time* and out of hypnosis— will be well worth the effort and will speed up your manifestations— rapidly.

By making a commitment to yourself to change your life for the better— you may have to clean up some of the things in your lifestyle that are causing you problems or keeping you in hypnosis. At first, making this commitment may not feel great. Whenever we take a stand and make a commitment what shows up are all the things that have become part of our lifestyle, in other words— habits. Eating protein every three hours and drinking more water and slowing down the caffeine and sugar may seem overwhelming at first—but— that is where t*he Mind Gate process* can help you.

A great visualization is seeing your-self in the mirror and then seeing yourself the way you really want to be. See yourself tipping a bottle of water to your lips with a big smile afterward— or riding a bicycle in one of those snazzy spandex cycling outfits. Let your emotional tone and the law of attraction do most of this for you. I've given you some ideas for staying out of hypnosis but even if you have a difficult time with that at first— *the Mind Gate process* will still work for you, it just depends on how fast you want it to work. When we make a commitment to change our life, it can seem overwhelming at first so— just start off with setting aside time to meditate and visualize and— maybe in a week or two you may feel good enough to work on the protein or the water or exercises I gave you earlier.

Remember always— be compassionate toward yourself because you've done the best you could with the information and programming you got and the most important thing is caring about the way you feel! If it *feels* good — that's good enough for now. Your *intention* must always be to *feel* good because—feeling good will *always* get you what you *really* desire in the core of your being! That's how the law of attraction works!

Chapter 8

Who and What We Really Are

*"Energy cannot be created or
destroyed, it can only be changed
from one form to another."*
-Albert Einstein

We live in an abundant universe, do we not? Look around. It is our *destiny* to thrive. We are not built to— nor ever have been— supposed to struggle through life. We have a *built-in mechanism* to create all the abundance, health and happiness we will ever need to be successful and thrive! This *built-in mechanism* has been present since and even before—our conception. It took a cell from our mother and a cell from our father and created a whole, multi-celled human being! It successfully created you! We are all *physical manifestations of an a*bundant universe and *abundance* is not only our birthright— but our very nature.

Did you know that— to make sure you were created, your biological father donated anywhere from 40 million to 1.2 billion sperm cells? But— it only took *one sperm cell* to fertilize your biological mother's egg—which then created— you! Nature is truly abundant and everything has been provided to guarantee us success as a species and as individuals. Our physical bodies have been taken apart and dissected by researchers and scientists throughout the years in an attempt to actually find this *creating mechanism.*

Every medical and chiropractic student has taken, as part of their studies, *human dissection* and— even though all the parts are there, none of us have ever found— the *thing* that once animated that body. So then—what is missing? My Human Dissection instructor would say—"What we found is 'no-thing'!" There are tissues and cells but *no-thing* that can be called the *life-force* or mechanism that creates life!

There is nothing or *no-thing* that can be seen all the way down to the tiniest of particles because— when the most powerful of electron microscopes is employed— there is only space, only potential, only possibility and— only energy! However, thanks to the science of quantum physics, we can *observe* this *creative mechanism* at work.

Energy and Creation

In1803, a physician and scientist by the name of Thomas Young, performed an experiment which changed the way we looked at the universe— both energy and matter— forever! Young's famous "double-slit" experiment demonstrated that matter (in this case— light) and energy can display characteristics of both waves and particles. Young had to overcome the century-old view— expressed in Sir Isaac Newton's "Optics"— that light is a particle. The quantum world had just opened up to us.

Fast forwarding—big time— to1998, another famous experiment took place—where an even bigger *game- changer* immerged— called the "electron observation experiment."

The experiment revealed that— by the very act of watching— the "observer" affects the quality— and the nature of the energy. So, basically— *matter and energy are the same thing*— energy!

"Everything is energy, that's all there is to it..."
-Albert Einstein

And, depending on what we put our attention or *focus* on— we will have an effect on how this energy behaves. When we put our attention on or *focus on* a thought or idea— we literally *force* the waves of energy to act or behave as *particles*. In other words—matter or physical things! We are able— through the act of a *sustained train of thought* on some *central idea* to be able to create *things* or *circumstances* to literally *manifest*— or— *show up* in our physical world. By using our imagination to create a visualization we are *impressing* a *thought-form* or *blueprint* onto or into the field of energy or *the formless* if you like. We are *forcing* our *will* onto *the force*! I like the idea of *the force* because, whatever our idea of God is— It is indeed a very strong energy or force and— it takes the religious connotations out of the equation.

"May the Force be with you"-Star Wars

Another analogy or metaphor I like to think about is from the "Star Trek" TV shows and movies. The *transporter device* (room) was able to dissemble matter (particles) into waves then reassemble the waves back into matter (particles) somewhere else, wherever the operator set (put his attention on) the coordinates for. This amazing device not only could do this in *present time* but could transport the Star Trek crew into another time— in the *future* or— in the *past*! WOW!

We have a similar device or *mechanism* that is built into us and— at this time it appears as if this *mechanism* may use *holographic-like* images to *impress* our ideas or thoughts onto the *unified field of consciousness* or— into the *universal field*. This *mechanism* and even how to use it— is only now just beginning to be understood by modern researchers— and probably— not any too soon.

It is *human consciousness* itself but— accessing it and learning how to direct it is— the trick. I don't believe that humans are the only creatures who have this *mechanism* because of the prolific amount of animals all over the planet but I do believe we humans have learned to— *suppress* this mechanism.

If we look closely at nature, even in the bleakest of environments like the frozen tundra of the South Pole we see abundance. National geographic did a several page story on the "Indomitable Snow Frogs" of the French Alps. These tiny little *Snow frogs* live, mate, lay eggs and birth tadpoles in near-freezing pools of water. In other words— they thrive. In other places on the planet there are pools of hot sulfur water where small fish and other creatures live and procreate and—they thrive! Everywhere on our planet there are animals and plants that thrive in the harshest of conditions.

They adapt in so many ways. Hibernation and adaptation in numerous ways ensures not only their survival but also their success as a species. Some will camouflage for protection and— some will camouflage to hunt. Our planet earth is literally *teaming* with life everywhere. It is truly abundant—in every sense of the word. Does it make sense to you that every species known to us humans comes with a—*built-in mechanism* for living and thriving but— humans somehow—have missed out on that?

Now, thanks to Hubble Telescope pictures we are discovering strange and amazing new galaxies and planets. There are stars, galaxies and solar systems that dance— explode and *bedazzle* us with their beauty. The pictures taken by the Hubble telescope— of galaxies and solar systems (and there are millions of them- solar systems that is- not pictures) are the *most* incredible and awesome light shows we could ever imagine. These *strange new worlds* and spectacular arrangements of star systems appear to go on and on. We'll eventually build an even more powerful telescope to see even further into space. What the Hubble is showing us is—there seems to be *no end* to the Universe! If that's not abundance— I don't know what is.

Scientists tell us that we live in a *holographic universe* and— our own brain processes information as images (quantum holography) like a holograph. A holograph by definition is a picture or one whole thing that has been created by one creator. We have access to all consciousness and are— a part of every other bit of consciousness throughout the universe.

Therefore, we as humans, have the ability and power to focus on literally anything and then —impress those focused thoughts like a *holographic image* onto that *field of consciousness* and then— assemble waves into particles or matter. I have no doubt there are other creatures that do this on some level for survival but— we humans are unique because—we create art! We are so powerful that we can even create heaven or hell depending on what we are putting our attention on!

"In a holographic world any *single* event is the result of all events in the universe; *events* as such have no self-existent reality. The universe is man's consciousness. It requires a comprehension beyond intellect"-D. Hawkins, M.D., Ph.D.

What I really want you to get is this—you are a part of the *cosmos*— a part of all creation and what's really exciting is that— as the Hubble telescope is showing us—the *universe* is expanding. This means that *human consciousness is expanding!* So, there is hope because there is indeed— a "flowering of human consciousness" as Eckhart Tolle says. We are, as a species beginning to *wake up*— to who and what we are!

Creation did not stop with the Earth. It is going on constantly. But who or what is doing the creation? It appears as if —*we are!* We are creating new resources (abundance) as we expand our consciousness! We are not *running out of stuff.* Yes, we are running out of oil but— we have much more abundant resources for power. The sun, the wind, the ground and sustainable agricultural crops that produce *pollution-free power* and new building materials are only just recently beginning to be used—and they are not limited!

Overpopulation

I would agree that we are producing an *abundance* of humans but— along with them will come— the motivation to create new ways to live, like space-stations or perhaps even other planets. I'm not burying my head in the sand here. I'm simply saying that we need to be *focusing* on possible solutions rather than the problems. The earth and the cosmos are so complex and abundant with resources that we are only beginning to uncover the abundance that we are all a part of. Through the sciences of quantum physics and neuroscience we are rapidly developing solutions to many of our so-called *problems*. We are definitely, as a civilization, learning to *think outside the box*— albeit we may still have a long way to go— before we come anywhere close to reaching our potential.

Quantum Physics

Quantum physics is a branch of science that deals with the sub-atomic world where matter is simply seen as discrete indivisible units of energy called *quanta*. There are five main areas represented in quantum theory:

1. Energy is not continuous, but comes in small but discrete units.
2. The elementary particles behave both like particles and like waves.
3. The movement of these particles is inherently random.
4. It is physically impossible to know both the position and the momentum of the particle at the same time. The more precisely one is known, the less precise the measurement of the other is.
5. The atomic world is nothing like the world we live in.

While at first glance this may seem like just another strange theory, it contains many clues to the fundamental nature of the universe and is more important than even Einstein's *theory of relativity* in the grand scheme of things (If any one thing at that level could be said to be more important than anything else). Furthermore, it describes the nature of the universe as being much different than the world we see.

"Anyone who's not shocked by quantum theory has not understood it."-Niels Bohr

With the use of quantum physics and quantum mechanics theories, which themselves are *ever-expanding* to deal with all the new information that comes out—on nearly a daily basis from some amazing physicists, biologists, neuroscientists and other researchers—a *working-model* is beginning to emerge. I believe that *working model* is—*the Mind Gate process* I've just outlined for you.

You will, with practice, rapidly learn how to use your Conscious mind as it was intended to be used and soon— will learn how to *dial-in* this technique and become— more effective and more accurate and create *exactly* what you want and— help everyone else on the planet and even those who have not arrived yet— at the same time!

What You Need To Know

This *working model* requires learning how the mind works and *accepting* who and what you are—and then— playing with your imagination while the law of attraction actually does the work. Many of us *Westerners* have a little more trouble than *Easterners*— with meditative practices. Due to such polarized cultural differences, we are just a little behind the curve on meditation so— *the Mind Gate process* will be a crash-course for some.

Effective meditation and visualization can be easily and nearly effortlessly mastered when done with *the process*— even if you are a beginner. If you were once under the age of eight you will learn this easily just like tying your shoes or riding a bike, it will all come back to you with a little practice. By thinking of and viewing our own physical bodies, the planet, our solar system and even consciousness itself as a hologram, we can more easily extrapolate or *intuit* that— there must be an energy source that can project an image into *formless matter* or *energy* that creates *formed matter. That energy source is the mechanism that is hardwired into us.*

A *hologram* is a *photographic record* produced by illuminating an object with coherent (clear or one-colored) light (as from a laser) and, without using lenses, exposing the film to light reflected from this object into a directed beam of coherent light. When interference patterns (Young's double-slit experiment) on the film are illuminated by the coherent light— a three-dimensional image is produced.

> "The term *hologram* refers to an image that is static and does not convey the dynamic and ever active nature of the incalculable enfolding's and unfolding's that movement by movement create our universe..." – "The Holographic Universe.

In the book that inspired the movie THE SECRET, "Financial Success Through Creative Thought or The Science Of Getting Rich" (1915), Wallace Wattles speaks of using our imagination in a *certain way* to impress a thought upon *formless substance (*the Force or Unified Field) to create an impression that will become matter or physical reality and this is how we manifest our world. Keep in mind that book was written around 1915!

But, Young's "double-slit" experiment demonstrated that particles can act like waves and vice versa in 1803! Has consciousness expanded from there? I do believe so, yes. Not that our species doesn't need even more work in consciousness expansion but, it is happening. This is a very exciting time we are living in. Karl Pribram's "Holonomic" model describes brain processing like this— "the brain appears to work as— and store information like a hologram." Beginning to sound a little like a *built-in mechanism* now?

Getting back to abundance for a moment— I believe that— real abundance is not only our birthright but is— in fact— what we do unless— our *intention* is to be *destructive*. In the positive state of creation or *intention* we *expand* our universe and everyone else's universe (the ripple effect & Butterfly effect). But, in the negative state of creation or *mal-Intention* we *contract* our universe— and— everyone else's universe as well— to a lessor or more degree.

In his book, POWER VS FORCE, and I am paraphrasing here…. Dr. David Hawkins explains that it is vital that the human race learn how to raise their consciousness by cultivating harmony and practicing compassion or we will eventually annihilate each other. He goes on to state very clearly that we, each and every one of us, affects the other and that our energy levels (emotional tones) have what he calls *attractor fields* that resonate with other *attractor fields* in a sort of holographic dance with each other and that the universe is actually— our collective *consciousness* being expressed as *energy*. In other words, the law of attraction will either be positive or negative and that *we are*— in fact— *the law of attraction— incarnate*!

"In a holographic universe the achievements of every individual contribute to the advancement and well-being of the whole"-David R. Hawkins, M.D., Ph.D.

"The idea that the physical body is just one more level of density, and the human energy field is itself a kind of hologram that has coalesced out of the interference patterns of the aura may explain both the extraordinary healing powers of the mind and the enormous control it has over the body in general"-Michael Talbot, "The Holographic Universe"

To be able to access and use this *mechanism*— so it will work for us (and everyone else on the planet) and—*not against* us— to attract or create what we want—we have to understand two things. We need to understand *what,* and not necessarily *who* we are and—we need to know how to use our *built-in mechanism* properly and with—*right intention.* Most people have been using their *mechanism* by default so— they have a mixture of good and bad experiences, leaning more or less one way or the other— depending on their Subconscious mind's programming. Neuropsychologists now estimate that at least 70% of our Subconscious mind's programming is — negative!

To create—deliberately— instead of *by default* requires some shifts in our perspective about the nature of reality and —this includes our reality about ourselves and the world we live in. Our paradigm or our model of what it takes to manifest our heart's desires will naturally shift when we accept a much broader view of ourselves. If we can embrace the discoveries from the science of quantum physics as well as some of the principles of the Tao or a better balance between *doing* energy and *being* energy there is absolutely— nothing that cannot be accomplished. However, we must always remember that the real power or— point of attraction behind all of this is our *state of mind* or our *emotional tone.*

Master the emotional tone scale by staying out of hypnosis during waking hours and practice *visualizing* and *feeling* — whatever makes you feel good— every day.

"May the Force be with you"-George Lucas

CHAPTER 9

Channeled

*"If we find ourselves with a desire that
nothing in this world can satisfy, the
most probable explanation is that we
were made for another world"*
- C.S. Lewis

*"We are travelers in time...our
energy has no boundary. We are
the projected image of God"*
-Dr. Mitchell Mays

Over the centuries there have been enlightened beings —
who have put down their ideas on paper, papyrus, wood or
stone for others to read and consider. None of these *writings*
are the *truth* or *gospel* for you. They are sign posts, pointing
the way to a higher truth. These enlightened human beings
shine a light, as if to say— "look over here— this is what I
have seen." You alone must find the path— *your* path. The
path you have chosen but perhaps may have long forgotten—
is always calling to you— in a still small voice.

Please read the following and then read it again— and if necessary— a third time until the meaning really *touches* a part of you inside. If it does not resonate with you on some level then dismiss it and just pay attention to how it *feels* to you as you read the words and consider what they imply.

It is very, very important for us to understand— not just *who* we are but— *what* we are if we are to become the *conscious* and *deliberate* creators that is our birthright. And then, once again we will take our rightful place in the universe. Refer back to this page as often as necessary until you own this fact. You are indeed as powerful and infinite as the universe itself because, You and I in fact— all of us— are the universe! I understand that this is a huge concept to wrap our heads around because very few of us are willing to accept that kind of responsibility *but* I tell you this—with all sincerity— you already are responsible but probably are not cognizant of this fact.

Quantum physics research and now neuroscience research confirms the notion that the *mystery schools* and *religions* throughout the ages have been telling us. That is— it is us (human beings) that wield the mighty force of creation itself! I believe it is critical that we accept the truth of this so we stop creating what we don't want. We need to let our children know that we know the truth about what they really are. I am, and you are a God among Gods!

I AM

I am— immortal. I do not exist as a leaf that springs to life only to wither and dry and fall from the tree when the winds turn cold and the sun grows further away.

I've existed long before time began. I am source. I am time, I am the Universe. I am love, I am war. I am life and sometimes I am a killer of life. I do not exist for you. I exist for myself.

I can carry your load for a while but if you wish me to be in servitude forever I will leave and I will hurt you because my life MUST be expressed. This is why I am here.

I love and protect and I do battle for that which I choose to protect and love. I am selfish. I do not sacrifice my life for others— nor ideals. I do not sacrifice my life for political goals nor for some patriotic allegiance to a state or country— nor for any tribe.

I am a warrior if I need to be and a lover all other times. Since love feels better than hate, I do not allow myself to hate because I always want to feel good. Anger is an emotion that is brought forth only when it becomes necessary when I or that that I love is in need of protection. It is a weapon of defense and never to be used to offend.

I use this weapon only rarely and always with temperance— I am not afraid to wield it when necessary. But use of it is inevitable when walking the earth plane.

In high places— it is convenient to speak of peace and love and I do so whenever I can— but down among the forces of society while peace is always a hope and a goal to strive for, it is fleeting in nature and therefore— must be cultivated by all who wish it manifest in their lives. That is reality on the earth plane.

Playing a role or *pretending* to be a man or woman of peace becomes an abomination known as a *people-pleaser*. Those who take this path, usually very early in life— initially as a coping and survival tool— will find it difficult to break its hold. It is seductive and has been birthed from the *dark side*. It will lead them into decisions and situations they will later, deeply regret. *People-pleasing*, when done habitually— is self-denied prostitution and this loathing of the self leads the individual into self-indulgence of every kind.

Therefore, exist for no man, woman or ideal—exist only for you. As the *authentic* you— love will come from you as water from an underground spring.

So become *authentic*— someone you may have never met. All of your power resides within your authentic self. You will then own your heritage.

Say to your-self often— "I exist for no one and everyone at the same time. I am you. I am an enigma. I pray for peace but always stand ready with the sword of truth— my truth

I am divinity living in a human body. I am life. I am vulnerable and violent at the same time. Do not trust me and do not forsake me.

I am the alpha and the omega. I am an enigma—I am a mystery and, as long as I see reality as a mystery and remain in that mystery— all the power of the Universe is mine to command".

"Is it not written, ye are Gods?"-John 10:34

A young Hindu student came to see his guru and bowed before him. The student's clothing was covered in dust and torn all over. He was bleeding from numerous cuts and scratches on his elbows, knees and face.

"What happened to you?" asked the guru.

"Is it not true that I am God, as you have been teaching?" the student replied.

"Yes, that is true, you are God", said his teacher. The student continued, "Well as I was walking on the road an elephant with a man riding on its back came running down the road toward me. The man was shouting to me—"get off the road, get off the road" as the elephant was coming very fast toward me. At first I thought, I should move off to the side of the road. Then I remembered your teachings and again I thought to myself— *since I am God, no harm will come to me because the elephant will surely stop for God.*

Just when the elephant was about to run over me it reached out with its great trunk and threw me off to the side of the road sending me tumbling in the dirt and the rocks.

"Yes, yes go on", encouraged his teacher.

"Well, if it is true that I am God, how come the elephant did not stop for me?" asked the student with all sincerity. The guru looked at his student with amusement of his obvious misunderstanding of the teaching.

"Why didn't you get off the road when God shouted at you from atop the elephant?"

When we awaken to *what* we are, we will have no choice except to embrace and accept that the whole of humanity is God and are all the same—yes, I said *the whole of humanity*— and all things that spring from the earth and the cosmos. Then we will understand and be able to use the awesome power we have available to us in the way that will give us what we want— which is really— what everyone else wants!

And not just embrace the idea of *Oneness* but accept the fact that *you* are completely responsible for *everything* in *your world*! It has been my experience that many people can accept the idea that they might be God—like a *piece* of apple pie is still *apple pie*— but when it comes to being *the one* who *made* the apple pie—it's a little more difficult to wrap your head around that kind of responsibility and power.

> "You are here to enable the divine purpose of the universe to unfold. That is how important you are!"-Eckhart Tolle

So then—what are we? We are divinity focused into a physical body. I tell my clients they are Divinity and not an Identity. We are a *divine* being—or *energy*—or *spirit*—a *presence* or *spark* or whatever else you would like to call it. We have a physical body but just like wearing a suit of clothing, we are no more that suit than we are the shoes on our feet. But many have come to believe that they are—less than—their clothing! Like an actor playing a part—our circumstances, job, career, profession, family, race, color and religion are not *what we* are—because *we* have been asleep.

> A student asked the Buddha, "Who are you, are you a God?" "No replied the Buddha—I am awake".
>
> "Reality is merely an illusion, albeit a very pleasant one."-Albert Einstein
>
> "We dream we are awake, having an experience that seems so real that we believe it is reality."-Dr. Mitchell Mays
>
> "You've been living in a dream world Neo…"-from the movie, "The Matrix"

THE DREAMER

You've been living in a dream world. You have been asleep
for—a very long time.

You dream of poverty, lack, sickness and even war.

You dream of violence and hatred and prejudice. You dream
of death and dying.

You dream that your brothers are your enemies. You dream of
being taken advantage of and that—there is not enough
to go around.

You dream of getting all you can and are always calculating
how you will be able to keep what you have from others.

You dream of others stealing from you—lying to you and
cheating you.

You have fearsome dreams—dreams of feeling guilty for just
being here.

You dream that you are not worthy or enough. You are
more than enough. You are everything—there is, but you
don't know that because—you are dreaming that you are
separate from—all that is.

You dream of worries and stresses. You dream your brothers
are taking things away from you and— you dream this
will make you less.

Nothing real can be taken from you.

You dream of failure and loss of control and there is no peace
in your dreams.

You dream of abandonment and that someone or something
holds the happiness— that is missing from your life.

You dream of grief, of loss and sadness. You dream of pain.

You dream of failure— but are afraid of success. You dream of deceit— and distrust even yourself.

You dream that your body and mind are betraying you. You dream you are mortal and that you will die.

You sleep...

All of your dreams of fear and loss come from believing you are something that you are not.

You are not any of the things or ideas that you think you are because— there are no such things as thoughts.

Thoughts are illusion— like your dreams. They are not real.

You let them in and accepted them as truth when you were new here because— they fascinated you.

In your new body and mind you were fertile soil for others to plant— their seeds of fear and guilt and despair.

But, you knew this would happen and you accepted that condition.

This was the game you wanted so very much to play.

Do you remember now? You agreed that you would focus your energy into physical matter— and become a human form.

You agreed that you would forfeit all memory of who and what you are.

This was the game you wanted so very much to play—and still do.

You agreed to come to this time and place and to be subjected to programming and belief patterns from your parents and tribe.

It is important to remember that— it was you who chose to play this game.

The game was explained in much detail and you agreed to travel this physical plane— enter into the maze— and play the game.

You were eager for this experience. And, when your physical body is all used-up and exhausted or when you tire of this game— and laughing after this grand experience, you will find your way back home to reflect— and rest— and perhaps, play again soon.

When you find yourself eventually— in this game of hide and seek— you will wake up to what you really are— and then you will claim the prize— your birthright— your power and your inheritance.

Are you ready?

You are not now— nor have you ever been— mortal. You have just been dreaming you are mortal.

You sleep…

It is now time to wake up. It is time to wake up from your dream.

And just because you are reading this— and just because— you are getting closer to waking up— this time you will remember— this has only been a dream—this time— you will remember.

And when you shed this physical body and re-emerge back into

Light-energy— this game— will end…

Do you remember now?

I'll give you words and processes to help you wake. And when you do— you will remember— and what a joyful moment that will be.

For now— the dreamer reads these words— but as you remember— it will be the opposite of what you now call "waking up" in your physical body.

The words I offer here for you, are words of comfort and are meant to help rouse you gently— but firmly from a bad dream.

The ones who drove you into your dream -world were dreaming also and were merely keeping their end of the agreement— with you.
No matter how it has appeared to you— they meant you no Harm— and in fact— love you very much.
They agreed, per your request, to play this game with you— the game you wanted to play.

Many of the words and beliefs they offered to you were meant for your protection— because of their own dreams of fear, violence and betrayal.

Their fears were great and so their words carried great fear which was shocking to your young mind. It was all these shocks that made you escape into your dream. You have been living their fears— do you remember now?

The joy that you are naturally— has been suppressed by your dreams of fear and guilt that were given to you when you were still innocent— but as long as you sleep— and as long as you dream that you are awake— the joy that you are will not be expressed fully and you will resist its energy.

The dreamer will not let it come to the surface. The dreamer resists— but not for long. The dreamer is afraid....

It is afraid if it releases the joy—then the joy will be gone— as if it were a limited resource....

The dreamer believes it can hold onto and keep the joy for the right moment.

It believes it will release the joy— when it has enough money, the right relationship, the right job, the right house, better health—and so it holds onto joy— keeping it safe in its hiding place until— the right time.

The dreamer has forgotten where it hid the joy. But, remember that this has always been a game—of hide and seek.

"The Dreamer" comes from a source that has been familiar to me all my life, like an invisible friend that children play with. I had completely forgotten about him for many years but now he whispers once again in my ear, oftentimes at 3:30 in the morning. As a child he comforted me when life was cruel and he played in the dirt with me. He sang to me at night— lulling me to sleep and held me when I was sad.

We have all had such *imaginary* companions but most of us have forgotten about them. They are still there and will come to us again— if we ask them to. Are they our guardian angels? Who knows— but what I do know is this. He has been there to lean on when I stumbled— and carry me when I could not walk.

Chapter 10

The Process In a Nutshell

"Our deepest fear is that we are powerful beyond measure"
-Marianne Williamson

So, waking up to who and what you are means accepting an awesome power. We are afraid of this power at first. We don't want to look at all the pain we have created but the pain we created was necessary— to get us to this point and to this time where we eventually can—surrender to it. To accept fully that we are made in the *image* of God and are the *creators* of our world is an awesome and seemingly terrible power that we must not shrink from but learn to embrace.

We must take our rightful place in the universe consciously as a God among Gods. I love this from Marianne Williamson because it speaks frankly and honestly to what we really are.

Our Deepest Fear

"Our deepest fear is not that we are inadequate.
Our deepest fear is that we are powerful beyond measure...

As we are liberated from our fear, our *presence* automatically liberates others."

BEFORE WE CAN MANIFEST INTENTIONALLY WE MUST:

- Accept the truth of *what we are.*
- Intend to keep our state of mind in the higher levels on the emotional tone scale.
- Learn to use our imagination *responsibly.*
- Learn how to change our *state of mind* as rapidly as possible until it becomes what we do— automatically.
- Stay out of hypnosis by eating protein, breathing and recognizing when a *negative* program is running.
- Take all the credit for all of our perceptions and experienced reality—all of it— the good and the bad and never blame anyone or anything again for our negative experiences.
- Forgive ourselves for our mistakes because we didn't know.
- Forgive others because we attracted them into our experience.
- Allow all manifestations we experience—resisting none of them because we created them all—remember?
- Turn the other cheek by taking our attention off anything we don't want in our experience.

The Mind Gate Exercise

1. Sit or recline in a darkened room with headset on or ear-buds in and music/sound on at low to medium volume. Make sure you will not be disturbed by anyone or anything. Set a timer for twenty minutes

unless you are able to go longer—holding your vision or good-feeling thoughts for at least sixty eight seconds.

2. Breathe deep into the abdomen for a few breaths then hold before breathing out more slowly than you breathed in for about five minutes. Allow your breathing to continue rhythmically after that.

3. Visualize, imagine or pretend that your vision is fulfilled and you are experiencing and *feel* the emotion that comes with that fulfillment or simply— be in a beautiful place of your choosing or— just listen to the music and *feel* the energy field of your body in your feet or hands and how amazing that is. If your mind wanders to anything negative—quickly pull your attention back to your vision, your good feelings or into your body's energy field.

4. When your visualization feels really good then you must hold that vision and feeling for at least sixty eight seconds then *anchor* the vision and good feelings by putting your thumb and forefinger together as you breathe in. See the vision and *feel* the feelings. Remember to incorporate as many of the five senses as you can while meditating, i.e. visual, auditory, touch, taste and smell.

5. Take your vision and good feelings with you in your day to day activities knowing that you are doing the work to deliberately raise your energy. Whenever possible, think of your vision as you touch your thumb and forefinger together. Your *anchor* needs to be used like a muscle. It becomes stronger and more effective with regular use.

"Skip over the how and the where and the when and the who—and just stay focused on the what and the why"- Esther Hicks as Abraham

SOME FINAL THOUGHTS...

I've explained, in great detail, the emotional tone scale which could be said as— *our state of mind scale* or *the mood scale* or *emotional feelings scale*. In other circles it is known simply as the Tone Scale. The emotional tone scale is simply about our state of mind. We now know from the works of Milton Erickson (Ericksonian Hypnosis)— Richard Bandler and John Grinder (neuro-linguistic programming or NLP) and Dr. John Kappas (Kappasinian Hypnosis) as well as many others, that our state of mind drives our behaviors.

Our behaviors are what attract people, things, situations or circumstances into our perceived reality. These emotional tones or moods come from our so-called thoughts— which for the most part come from our Subconscious mind. These *thoughts* create responses in the body called *emotions*.

For many years psychotherapists have taught that if you are *feeling* sad or depressed then all you have to do is change your thoughts to happy thoughts. And, that is true— however, if you are deeply unhappy and don't know how to break the vicious cycle of *negative* feedback loops between your body and mind you can waste years and years on a therapists couch before *waking up* and moving up the tone scale deliberately. Or worse, waste many life-times before coming to the conclusion that you are your own worst enemy— and if you want to be happy— then you have to decide to be so.

I say *waking up* because when we get stuck in an emotional tone— we are actually asleep— not unconscious delta sleep but a form of simulated sleep—called hypnosis or tranced. As a result, if we are feeling un-Happy or any other *negative* feeling (negative feedback loop) we become more and more— suggestible— to negative influences in our environment. In other words, you can easily get stuck in a *negative* emotional tone. And like a radio station, it can play on and on—if you don't know how to change the channel.

I have endeavored to illustrate exactly what that mechanism is and how it works in Chapter 3: The Mind Gate.

In Chapter 4: Mastering the Emotional Tone Scale, I went over in great detail— how to control that mechanism to make it work for you and that it has levels or channels— like a television or radio. By now, you are learning that it is a matter of tuning into the right channel or frequency—to the station you want.

Your perfect radio station or television show is just waiting for you to find the right frequency— and when you do— you will automatically create your life the way you always wanted and—dreamed it could be. Just be persistent and keep practicing *the Mind Gate process* —remembering that it is a natural process and that you *can* learn it.

Make a commitment to your-self to stay out of hypnosis— except when you want to be. Always enter the Mind Gate with the best of intentions— and the best will always come back to you.

In the final analysis— we are mental, physical and spiritual beings —we are multi-dimensional and—we are *enigmas*. You have to pick or develop some philosophy or theology that *feels* right or good to you—or develop your own— whatever that may be.

There are no *answers* "out there." There are only *possibilities* "in here"— inside the *energy-field* that we are. I can only hope that I have given you some help and—perhaps some positive guidance on your journey—and be able to shine a light and say—"look over here—this is what I see."

You are— without a doubt— an *immortal* and *divine* time-*traveler*— in the truest sense of the idea— and perhaps— long after you have read these words— may you know at last— the truth of —*what you really are!* I honor the divinity that you are.

Namaste,
Dr. Mitchell Mays

RESOURCES

Professional Hypnotism Manual-John Kappas, Ph.d.
The Power of Now, A New Earth, Stillness Speaks-
Eckhart Tolle
A Course in Miracles-Helen Schucman &William Thetford
The Science of Becoming Oneself- H. Saraydarian
The Book of Secrets, Meditation- Osho
Tao Te Ching- Lao Tzu
Financial Success Through Creative Thought or The Science
of Getting Rich- Wallace D. Wattles
The Impersonal Life- Joseph S. Benner
The Miracle of Mindfulness, No Death, No Fear, Going
Home- Thich Nhat Hanh
The Spontaneous Healing of Belief, Deep Truth, The Divine
Matrix, The God Code- Gregg Braden
The Gnostic Gospels of Jesus- Marvin Meyer
Ask and It Is Given, The Astonishing Power of Emotions,
The Vortex, The Law of Attraction, The Amazing Power
of Deliberate Intent, Sarah Book 1- Esther and Jerry
Hicks- The Teachings of Abraham
The Secret- Rhonda Byrne
The Science Behind The Secret- Travis S. Taylor, Ph.D.
Holy Bible-King James and New International Versions
The Biology of Belief- Bruce Lipton, Ph.D.

Spontaneous Evolution- Bruce H. Lipton, Ph.D. & Steve
  Bhaerman
Ageless Body, Timeless Mind: The Quantum, The
  Spontaneous Fulfillment of Desire- Deepak Chopra, M.D.
Re-Inventing Yourself- Dick Sutphen
A Practical Guide to Past Life Regression- Florence Wagner
  McClain
You Are the Answer- Michael J. Tamura
The Science of Mind, How to Change Your Life- Dr.Ernest
  Holmes
The Power of Decision- Raymond Charles Barker
The Disappearance of the Universe, Your Immortal Reality-
  Gary R. Renard
Soul Prints- Marc Gafni
The Tibetan Book of the Dead- Robert A. F. Thurman
The Prophet- Kahlil Gibran
Power vs Force, I Reality and Subjectivity, Discovery of the
  Presence of God, Truth vs Falsehood, The Eye of the I-
  David R. Hawkins, M.D., Ph.D.
Molecules of Emotion- Candace B. Pert, Ph.D.
Conversations With God- Neil Donald Walsh
You Can Heal Your Life- Louise L. Hay
The Holographic Universe- Michael Talbot
Courageous Souls- Robert Schwartz
Radical Forgiveness- Colin C. Tipping
Breaking the Habit of Being Yourself- Dr. Joe Dispenza
What the Buddha Taught- Walpola Rahula
The Power of Your Subconscious Mind- Joseph Murphy, Ph.D.
The Magic of Believing- Claude M. Bristol
The Miracle Man- Morris Goodman & Pat Garnett
The Paleo Diet- Loren Cordain, Ph.D.
Count Your Blessings- Dr. John F. DeMartini

No Attachments No Aversions- Lester Levenson
Your Body's Many Cries for Water- F. Batmanghelidj, M.D.
Quantum- Jim Al-Khalili
Love is the Answer- Gerald G. Jampolsky, M.D.
Living In Love With Yourself- Barry A. Ellsworth
A Return To Love, Everyday Grace- Marianne Williamson
The Seat of the Soul- Gary Zukav
John Bradshaw On: The Family, Reclaiming Virtue- John Bradshaw
Soul Psychology- Joshua David Stone, Ph.D.
Many Lives, Many Masters, Messages From the Masters- Brian Weiss, M.D.
Affirmations, The Force, The Secrets of Life- Stuart Wilde
The Butterfly Effect, The Travelers Gift- Andy Andrews
The Bhagavad-Gita- Barbara Stoler Miller
The Power of Perception- Marcus Bach
The True Power of Water- Masaru Emoto
Seth Speaks- The Eternal Validity of the Soul- Jane Roberts
Excuse Me, Your Life Is Waiting- Lynn Grabhorn
American Buddha- Stuart Mooney
Flow- Mihaly Csikszentmihalyi
The Code 10 Intentions for a Better World- Tony Burroughs
Inspiration, The Power of Intention, Manifesting Your Destiny - Dr. Wayne Dyer
Care of the Soul- Thomas Moore
The Souls Code-James Hillman
Future Shock, The Third Wave-Alvin Toffler
How To Choose Your People-Ruth Minshull
Wikipedia